PATRICK IRELAND:

LABYRINTHS, LANGUAGE, PYRAMIDS, AND RELATED ACTS

Russell Panczenko, Curator
with an essay by Jan van der Marck

Elvehjem Museum of Art
University of Wisconsin–Madison
Madison, Wisconsin
1993

A catalogue of the exhibition *Patrick Ireland: Labyrinths, Language, Pyramids, and Related Acts* organized by Russell Panczenko and held November 14, 1992 through January 10, 1993 at the Elvehjem Museum of Art, University of Wisconsin–Madison

Cover:
Labyrinth for the Elvehjem Museum of Art, 1992
Pencil and gouache on paper, 45 3/16 x 169 5/8 in.
Gift of the artist, 1992.359

CONTENTS

FOREWORD

Patrick Ireland: Labyrinths, Language, Pyramids, and Related Acts is the first attempt to review the broad range of work in the visual arts produced by this wonderfully creative individual. Brian O'Doherty is very well known in contemporary art circles; his penetrating insights into the work of visual artists since the 1960s have had a wide and profound impact. Less well known is the fact that O'Doherty, a.k.a. Patrick Ireland, has also had a long and successful career as a practicing artist.

Almost all previous exhibitions of Ireland's work have consisted of individual performances or site-specific installations or have concentrated on single concepts, such as the Portrait of Duchamp series. The one comprehensive exhibition, *Patrick Ireland, Drawings 1965–1985*, presented at the National Museum of American Art in 1986, concentrated on a single medium. This publication documents the exhibition presented at the Elvehjem Museum of Art from November 14, 1992 through January 10, 1993 and, like the exhibition, encompasses works produced by the artist between 1964 and 1992. Included are conceptual pieces, wordworks, drawings, sculpture, multimedia objects, and two installations, the Elvehjem labyrinth which was first conceived in the late 1960s but not executed until the Elvehjem exhibition, and the site-specific Rope Drawing #98. Several of the works included in the exhibition and this catalogue had never been exhibited or published. A somewhat abbreviated and altered version of the Elvehjem exhibition was presented from April 18 to June 20, 1993 at P.S. 1 in Long Island City. It also included a site-specific rope drawing, #99, which is not documented here.

The exhibition checklist, accompanied by a black-and-white illustration of each work, is not organized according to the chronology of the individual objects; rather it has been first subdivided into the categories used by the Patrick Ireland himself, in order to preserve and document this conceptual framework. The objects within each category, however, have been listed in chronological order. We have attempted to present the categories chronologically based on the earliest work in each one. The caveat here is that many of the categories overlap in time and several of them remain open with the artist returning, sometimes many years later, to develop their underlying concepts further.

Still, for this curator, steeped in traditional art historical methods, chronology remains an important tool in the effort to understand an artist's development. Thus the organization of the color plates differs significantly from that of the checklist; these are presented in strict chronological sequence without reference to the categories, and each one is intended to represent an important development in the artist's career. The plates begin with *Kip's Bay* of 1964, the earliest of Ireland's works to be included in the exhibition, and end with *Omphalos* and the *Labyrinth for the Elvehjem*, the two installations which were site specific to the museum. The latter two works have been more extensively documented with photographs because of their temporary natures.

The present catalogue includes an excellent introductory essay by Jan van der Marck, chief curator and curator of twentieth-century painting and sculpture at the Detroit Institute of Arts, and I am grateful for his gracious collaboration. The catalogue also publishes, many for the first time, a selection of Patrick Ireland's letters to scholars and colleagues in which he speaks openly about the ideas he explored in his art. These are an important primary source of information and the only real key to understanding this very complex body of work. The Elvehjem's exhibition and the present publication were not intended to be the complete study of Ireland's work which badly needs to be done. However, we hope that this project, by inspiring others to fill in the gaps, make corrections, and rethink developments will serve as a first step toward such a study.

As with all such exhibitions and publications, many individuals contributed to their successful completion. The *Labyrinth for the Elvehjem* was expertly constructed to the artist's specifications by Tim Coughlin, John Herman, Bruce Marble, Jerry Niesen, Joe Reitmair, and Ray Wahl of the University of Wisconsin–Madison's Physical Plant. Bruce Conover and Rick Hards, recent graduates of the Department of Art at the University of Wisconsin–Madison and artists in their own right, selflessly assisted Patrick Ireland with the installation of *Omphalos*, Rope Drawing #98.

I should also like to acknowledge the efforts of museum staff members who participated in this project. Particularly indispensable was registrar Lucille Stiger, who packed the works for this exhibition in New York City and supervised their installation at the Elvehjem. Assistant director for administration Corinne Magnoni effectively coordinated practical and financial matters, while accountant Lori DeMeuse kept diligent records of the myriad and complex transactions which inevitably accompany such an enterprise.

I also want to express my appreciation to Greg Anderson of The Photographic Media Center for photographic documentation of the exhibition, Earl J. Madden of University Publications for the catalogue design, Linda Kietzer of University Publications for coordination of production, and Patricia Powell of the Elvehjem staff for editing the catalogue and seeing it through publication.

Funding for the exhibition and its documentary catalogue came from discretionary funds generously provided to the Elvehjem by Christin Clark Cleaver, Evjue Foundation, Inc./ The Capital Times, Grace M. Gunnlaugsson, and Gavena C. Vickery.

I also want to acknowledge the kindness of the lenders to the exhibition: Charles Cowles Gallery, Renato Danese, Patrick Merla, Barbara Novak, and Jan van der Marck.

Finally, but most importantly, I wish to acknowledge the most generous and gracious hospitality and cooperation of Brian O'Doherty and his wife Barbara Novak. They unselfishly shared their ideas, opened private records, and patiently answered the many and sometimes naive questions that I posed. Thanks to their belief in scholarship and dedication to the arts, I gained a better appreciation and understanding not only of Patrick Ireland and his work but also of art of our time.

Russell Panczenko
Director
Elvehjem Museum of Art

Its retrospective nature and judicious selection made this exhibition the perfect occasion to advance a better understanding of Patrick Ireland's debt to Brian O'Doherty and Brian O'Doherty's relation to artists preceding and surrounding him. Patrick Ireland is the creator of meditative spaces of a Euclidian order tenuously defined by the optical coincidence of vertically, diagonally, and horizontally suspended ropes and floor-to-ceiling rectangles, trapezoids, and triangles painted on the ambient walls. Brian O'Doherty is the author of art criticism, filmmaker and teacher of film history, civil servant at the country's premier arts-granting agency, and recently acknowledged novelist. Even as such abundance of talent and the ability to function in multiple roles commands respect, professional purists, no doubt in self-protection, look askance at artists suspected of not devoting themselves to their art full time. Conversely, in the work-a-day world, the making of art is neither encouraged nor rewarded. That leaves O'Doherty/Ireland vulnerable on both ends.

Such a dilemma invites a new paradigm, i.e., that of the modern artist who claims art status even for enterprises skirting the making of art proper. At an early age, Brian O'Doherty, a budding painter in the figurative style growing up in a family of doctors, struck a Faustian bargain when he opted for the medical profession and went off to University College, Dublin. By surrendering the short-term goal of a career in art he aspired to the broader one of turning his life into a series of simultaneous and successive strategies with art as the primary objective. In this he is typical of an era that has made similar allowances for the likes of Albert Schweitzer and Marcel Duchamp, John Cage and Joseph Beuys.

In our age of specialization and certification, there is a tendency to frown upon the exercise of multiple talents. Versatility in more than one art, to professional watchdogs, smacks of amateurism, lack of commitment, or self-delusion. The opposite, in all likelihood, is true though art's unfortunate commodification in our time favors its single-focus practice and production. Throughout history the gifted have proudly paraded their abilities in seemingly unrelated fields of endeavor, matching poetry, painting, music, and science with soldiering, diplomacy, agriculture, and commerce. The Dada movement, three quarters of a century ago, introduced and hence sanctioned the intersecting and overlapping of the arts with other arts and life itself. Theo van Doesburg, the painter and founder of De Stijl, was a valued contributor of poetry to Dada magazines, a theoretician and educator with an encompassing media embrace characteristic also of Schwitters, Arp, and Richter.

In Dada's spirit, Fluxus, now thirty years ago, aggressively scrambled the hallowed notions that separated the arts, robbing music of its sound, words of their meaning, painting of its sensuousness, and sculpture of its traditional forms and materials. Fluxus proposed that as the drip of water could be music, so thought could be sculpture, slow movement dance, and vowels poetry. John Cage's gathering of mushrooms joins Marcel Duchamp's breeding of dust while anticipating Joseph Beuys's conversations with a coyote as virtual art. George Maciunas, the Proudhon of Fluxus, fought city inspectors and real-estate interests to ensure affordable housing for artists in the part of town that came to be known as SoHo. It is no less farfetched to assign art status to Maciunas's organizing fifteen artists' co-ops than it is to accept Beuys's founding of a political party based on plebiscite as "sculpture."

When trying to establish a context for O'Doherty/Ireland's activities in and between the fields of visual perception, educational television, art criticism, pictorial notations, environmental installations, political actions, and governmental consultation and draw a contemporaneous comparison, then Fluxus comes to mind. The artists identified with that movement bore no loyalty to traditional media, threatened existing value systems, were process instead of product-oriented, and rejected the notion of professionalism. Yet O'Doherty/Ireland never belonged to, was seen as, or considered himself an exponent of Fluxus.

As far as labels go, Brian O'Doherty accepts that of a postminimalist, interested in lines, grids, numbers, and systems. Historically, six years before his 1972 name change, O'Doherty was in the thick of conceptual experiment with Sol LeWitt, Eva Hesse, Dorothea Rockburne, Mel Bochner, Robert Smithson, and Dan Graham. But whereas his work was formally related to that of those one-time friends, his accomplishments of the last thirty years show a broader aesthetic kinship with Dada and Fluxus. In O'Doherty's phenomenological approach, slant on reality, and choice of repertory, Duchamp and Richter, Rauschenberg and Cage loom larger than the postminimalists chronicled by Lucy R. Lippard in her *Six Years: The Dematerialization of the Art Object from 1966 to 1972.*

This exhibition started out with a number of "gestures," dating from 1964 to 1972 for the most part. Properly understood, gestures belong to the temporary realm of the theater as they are made with an audience in mind and survive in photographs, material relics, and the memories of those in attendance. In 1913 Marcel Duchamp mounted a bicycle wheel on a kitchen stool for his own amusement, and in 1914, Arthur Cravan, from a fashionable lectern, treated his listeners to random pistol shots, insults, and profanities. With the advent of Fluxus, half a century later, such gestures solidified into concert performances that bore scant resemblance to music and enigmatic objects most viewers would hesitate to call art.

The Critic's Boots bear an uncanny resemblance, in spirit and appearance, to the props and relics of Happenings and Fluxus performances. Literally, they are the boots in which O'Doherty crisscrossed Manhattan to cover the gallery scene. The newsprint with which they are *covered* (same word!) are the very reviews he wrote for *The New York Times*. The critic O'Doherty collected those reviews in *Object and Idea* (1967); the artist O'Doherty did something more radical and anarchic with the same materials, playing down his importance as a critic and pressing the material evidence of his gainful employment into the service of art. Because O'Doherty felt uneasy about wearing two hats in a world that respects one or the other, but rarely both, *The Critic's Boots* came out of the closet for the first time in this exhibition.

Not surprisingly, O'Doherty has mined his medical training, including his postgraduate studies in the physiology of perception, for art subjects and ideas. The *Five Senses* (1965–72) and *Between Categories* (1957–68), both in this exhibition, attest to it. But beyond these direct forays into past interests and experiments, O'Doherty brings a scientific attitude and probing intellect, as well as historic literacy and aesthetic awareness to everything he touches. His highly original use of codes, electronic and linguistic, to impart concrete information through abstract means, resulted in two works of signal importance, *Portrait of Marcel Duchamp* (1966–67) and the *Ogham Series* (1967–71) of drawings and sculptures.

Portrait of Marcel Duchamp, unlike any portrait ever made in that it enshrines and through an electric impulse simulates the continued beating of the deceased's heart, is the slightly perverse tribute to an artist who claimed for the brain (and not the heart) creative functions formerly entrusted to the hand. Joseph Masheck, in his definitive critique of O'Doherty's *Electrocardiographic Portrait of Marcel Duchamp* (*Arts* 51, no. 5 [1976]: 108–109), left out that Duchamp had worn his heart on his sleeve, in a manner of speaking, and that *Coeurs Volants*, Duchamp's optically active blue and red heart shapes reproduced on the cover of *Cahiers d'Art XI* 1- 2 (1936), and reissued as a "Fluttering Hearts" poster by the Moderna Museet, Stockholm in 1961, could very well have been the younger artist's incentive. Masheck does suggest, though, a connection between the "found" line of the electrocardiogram and the string and rope that would preoccupy O'Doherty in his later spatial constructions. To facilitate that leap, however, the artist has offered us the comfort of a bridge in his ogham drawings and sculptures.

In 1967, Brian O'Doherty began a series of polished aluminum columns with inverted *W* contours on which surfaces were marked by discrete horizontal incisions running from top to bottom and reflecting one another and the viewer. Those columns, and the drawings reflecting the incisions, derive from the fifth-century Gaelic sign system called ogham, a simplified linear adaptation of the twenty letters in the Roman alphabet. O'Doherty chanced upon the ogham script at a time reductive strategies and serialism were in vogue. It was also the time he wrote a discerning essay on Hans Richter, analyzing the Dadist's serialism in cinematographic images, and befriended Morton Feldman (sometimes recruited by Fluxus) whose serialism in music he admired.

In 1984 Ireland/O'Doherty commented on that era:

> Back in 1967, I wanted to get three vectors crossing: the conceptual, serialism, and language. For this task I boiled down my verbal culture to three words and an obsolete sign language expressed in a perfect serial system. The words were ONE, HERE, NOW. . . . ONE obviously had to do with unity, the Absolute. HERE had to do with position, thus the ghost of composition. NOW collapsed past and future into the present. ("Wordless Images/Imaged Words" *Poetry East* 13/14, 1984)

This transliteration of the Holy Trinity shows up O'Doherty's rootedness in Catholicism but deeper yet, as for all Irish, is a pagan, Gaelic substratum nurturing the imagination. Such sense of connectedness made O'Doherty decide to change his name from Brian O'Doherty to Patrick Ireland.

Name Change in this exhibition documented, in the customary contemporaneous format of photograph and text, Brian O'Doherty's adoption of the name Patrick Ireland "until such time as the British military presence is removed from Northern Ireland and all citizens are granted their civil rights." This 1972 event occurred before a small audience and the actor was the artist himself. Ideologically it ranks as "body art," generally considered an exacerbation of "concept art," but it might just as well be related to Fluxus and, specifically, to its blood-and-guts-spilling Viennese wing which garnered headlines as early as 1970. The suggestion of death and mutilation addressed one of art's last taboos head-on. Viewed from yet another angle, one sees a Paulinian conversion scenario played out in this transfiguration of the noncommitted outsider into the ardent patriot covered by the bloody flag of his country.

Two of the most potent ideas/images which O'Doherty/Ireland has contributed to the iconographic storehouse of twentieth-century art are the labyrinth and the rope drawing. Both were dramatically executed in this exhibition. In 1967 O'Doherty presented a labyrinth at Finch College which, by his own admission, was inspired by the Saint Brigid's Cross, the traditional Irish weaving pattern. Labyrinthine shapes, like grids, had favored form status in the late 1960s and early 1970s. One can find them in the work of Tony Smith, John Willenbecher, Richard long, Dennis Oppenheim, Charles

Simonds, Alice Aycock, and Richard Fleischner, but Brian O'Doherty's is the first postminimalist labyrinth on record.

A relative latecomer to the maze, Robert Morris, whose 1974 *Labyrinth* derives from the convoluted stone mazes set into the floors of pilgrims' basilicas (another medieval source), is sometimes given inventor's credits because of the compelling but also intimidating nature of his creation. Morris's labyrinth was actually executed in Philadelphia in 1974 with a later version in the Gori sculpture park near Pistoia. O'Doherty's had to wait until 1990 when a small version was executed at the Charles Cowles Gallery, and 1992 when an even larger version at the Elvehjem gave us a hint of what the ultimately intended outdoor labyrinth will look like.

O'Doherty/Ireland's best known and most enduring accomplishment is the rope installation. Its incentives were the "Concept of the Labyrinth as a Straight Line," a notion the artist pursued ever since he started drawing labyrinths, and the linear configuration of the ogham script. A direct visual connection can be made between those groupings of short vertical or diagonal dashes and the first and relatively simple rope installations of 1973. With minimal means Ireland achieved results that over the years have become richer and more complex.

Ropes were strung between floors, walls, and ceilings in gridlike formations. Color entered as a sign system to differentiate one rope from another. Because he considers it the least rational of entities, Ireland asks himself the question of how he can control color, as he controls line, and develop it as structure.

Thus, color applied to walls monochromatically or in binary hues, evenly or in spots and blotches, all over or in the shape of a screen, window, or gate, is framed and recruited in the service of architectural illusion through a razor's edge articulation of tautly strung vertical, horizontal, and oblique ropes. Yet, color and ropes programmed to merge and complement one another do not form the intended single gestalt until the beholder physically penetrates their space and the mind's eye concentrates on the points of reference that will reveal their coordinates.

As comparisons have been made between Ireland's and Sol LeWitt's wall drawings, it is necessary to emphasize their fundamental difference. At the time Ireland executed his first rope drawings at 113 Greene Street, in 1973 a doubtlessly three-dimensional installation, Sol LeWitt drew monochrome lines and arcs on white gallery walls without utilizing the virtual art space between them. Ireland's first painted room, *Camera*, 1978, at the School of Visual Arts, divided the walls into discrete chromatic patterns in a manner that anticipated Sol LeWitt's later wall treatments. But, the most recent works in that artist's 1978 MOMA retrospective went only as far as providing varied colored backgrounds for different linear configurations. The architectural treatment of walls and the space between those walls with the sole means of rope, string, line, and color is Ireland's invention.

Fascinated by space and the systems with which it can be mapped or plotted, Ireland has hung ropes from imaginary sky hooks, has stood ropes upright with the ease of a fakir, has pitched nomads' tents of gently folding oblique lines, and has sketched fleeting perspectives that struck this viewer as the visual equivalent of an echo chamber. Percept keeps concept in a tenuous balance and the wanderer is enticed to locate where the real merges with the ideal in these illusory precincts. Not unlike a spider patiently watching its prey, the artist forces those who enter his environment to play his game by seeking perfect visual alignment with the web of his construction. While it may be true that control over form, color, and shape is every artist's ambition, for Ireland that emphatically includes control over the spectator, physically engaged and mentally caught in his labyrinthine spaces.

Omphalos, created at the Elvehjem Museum of Art, is Ireland's most recent version of the rope drawing installation. Its title, *Navel* in Greek, signifies, according to the artist, that "everything fell into place from the center." The most famous *Omphalos* was a navel-shaped altar or tombstone in Apollo's oracular shrine in Delphi, thought to be the center of the world. Ireland's environments, like so many amphitheaters, tend to have a preferred optical and acoustical center, requiring the visitor to hold still in one spot, from which to survey the sides and center in a 180–degree arc. *Omphalos* is conceived and perceived from that center. There, on a few square feet, the viewer steps into the artist's shoes, sets eyes on the artist's vision, and, in one fell swoop, makes that vision his own.

Jan van der Marck
Chief Curator and Curator
of Twentieth-century Art
The Detroit Institute of Arts
January, 1993

LETTERS FROM THE ARTIST

Letter to Janet Kardon
Director, Institute of Contemporary Art, Philadelphia
September, 1975

Why labyrinths? Well, there are the obvious things. After passing through, you have the illusion you understand something. And the difficulties of the process are always partly redeemed by the confidence that a solution is there, immediately visible if you could levitate yourself. The labyrinth with no solution, the Kafkaesque labyrinth, is a cruel invention, though I suppose it's closer to real life than the classic labyrinth, which is always an idealization of meaning. If you only knew, it would all make sense.

My interest in labyrinths has nothing to do with all this though. The labyrinth's content is so oppressive it has to be tuned down. I was surrounded by the labyrinth idea as a kid in Ireland, where you never get straight answers, you always get bent answers. Partly as a reaction, I suppose, I was very strong on concrete ideas and things (in 1967) and very much against curves. You're always slipping off curves. Also the labyrinth idea may have come from the grid of the chessboard and the paths inscribed on it by the pieces. If you trace the movements of, say, knight and bishop through a game, they look arbitrary and meaningful, which is a nice look if you can get it. I did a number of things on the movements of the pieces.

I wanted a very clear idea of a labyrinth, like a formal garden. While in it, you could still see the whole pattern, which was complex only if you wanted to make it so. I designed a labyrinth with an obvious center and easy routes to it for one of Elayne Varian's shows at Finch College. It was just a few feet high, which would make you Gulliver. You could see the ways to go, but not step over; you could also see the other people in the maze. So you'd have the overview but still be time-bound to your single corridor. This would put together the dislocation you have in a labyrinth where your head is always in advance of or behind your body. All the turns were right angles, no U-turns. I clarified a motif on a St. Brigid's Cross—a kind of cartwheel that can generate an infinite system. It's very simple, but once you lost the idea you'd be lost.

I did some flat labyrinths on mirrors to go on the wall or on the floor and a piece which floated a labyrinth in air, reflecting its mirrored insides in a mirror below. The outside was opaque and dense to give an idea of weight. Seeing the reflection inside was like breaking open a lump of granite and finding a perfect mirror on the inside of each piece. The horizontal design was simple, the complexities were all vertical. You could follow them down like a well until they turned green.

I did lots of drawings but didn't finish many pieces. Some dealt with the labyrinth as a straight line idea. Going along a straight line, with your eyes closed and turning by quarters clockwise and counter-clockwise, you get lost. You've got to go on other senses. I straightened out the Hampton Court labyrinth. I was also doing structural "plays" then, generating movement on a grid with words. I did one on the Hampton Court labyrinth and, as far as I remember, a few on the straight line idea.

I wanted to make labyrinths very easy, to diminish the urgency of a solution and to emphasize a rather lax process. You could get there in lots of ways and when you got there it wasn't all that interesting. Mine weren't authoritarian or concerned with "ingenuity." What was there was there, including you. I'd have liked to have cut one of these labyrinths into an Irish bog, which is a natural place for it, but there was a rush to the landscape at that time; to go with it would have been wrong for my work then.

If you've any other questions, please let me know. By the way, all these pieces were done in 1967/68.

This letter was published in "Janet Kardon Interviews Some Modern Maze-makers," *Art International* 20 (April-May 1976): 68.

Letter to Dorothy Walker
Art Critic, Dublin, Ireland
December, 1984

Since you have so bravely accepted a short deadline for a catalogue essay, I feel I should be giving you more help—were we closer in space we'd be having many conversations about the work. I don't know how much you have in your files, but I have the whole panorama of rope drawings in my head (since this catalogue will be confined to rope drawings, I guess the rest can be tackled when we get to the broad acres of a retrospective, should time be kind to us both). So since I can see the works on my own internal screen, as well as feel their different vistas and spaces in my body's memory, I hope it will be helpful to share some thoughts about rope drawings 1 through 73 (which this forthcoming one, *Purgatory*, will be, unless I rush out and do another in January).

The first drawing was the grid you reproduced in your article in *The Arts in Ireland* years ago. That in turn came from drawings of grids I did in the late sixties arising out of the ogham drawings. In these (15 x 15 grids) the number of strokes for the vowels (one to five) was turned into lengths (one to five spaces on the grid, each described by a different color). The grids then, could be read (broad and slender, as we learned in school). This led in 1970 to *Vowel Grid*, laid out on the ground with colored tape and performed, i.e. two walkers (one north-south; the other east-west). Patrick (Murphy) has a photograph of a performance of this at the Fogg Museum. It was first done in 1970. Translating the sixties' drawing into actual space, using ropes as lines, opened up the joyous exhilaration of drawing in space, placing any line in the air exactly where I wanted it, finding its placement through trial and error just as you do when drawing on a page, the line often suspended by almost invisible nylon thread.

Of the early drawings, the one I learned most from, the one that clarified for me a whole vocabulary of color and line, was *One Drawing in Two Rooms* at the Los Angeles County Museum in 1975. Two continuous sets of seven ropes fanned out from behind your head as the drawing passed through a doorway. The seven colors of the spectrum were randomly distributed on each set of seven ropes on either side of the doorway. Another set of seven ropes/colors crossed these to produce two wing-like grids, triangular in shape—all on one slanting plane that cut through the space obliquely. From one side of the gallery all the colors were fully visible; where they crossed made a veritable textbook of how color behaves on lines, particularly where two lines/colors crossed. To my astonishment you could make a red go back and a yellow come aggressively forward, etc. In other words, a line of color could be coached into paradox and contradiction. From the other side, silhouetted against the light-washed wall, the ropes were black and easily locatable. The work looked very different from the multiplicity of viewpoints available. As people rooted the back of their necks to the place where the lines crossed over from one gallery to the other and radiated out as they looked over their shoulders, it referred (discreetly, I think) to Leonardo's designs for flight.

This central node of the piece had a tremendous energy. One other very important thing happened: people eventually came to perceive it not so much as an art work, but as a *place* that happened *through* them. They came and stayed and behaved according to cues implicit in the work that had not been fully visible to me. This gentle, nonauthoritarian fusion of spectator and artwork in a specific—always specific—situation was a revelation to me; it also got rid of the whole sad dialectic of the rooted spectator and the obstinate artwork imprisoned in its frame or paralyzed on its pedestal—the "I – It" number. Most people usually refer to all this in my work as "perceptual," and some even call it my stuff "perceptual art," whatever that is. Though perception is obviously as much a part of seeing art as it is of eating your breakfast, I'm uncomfortable with the term. It suggests an isolation of a faculty rather than the profound reformation of your assumptions by a complex dialectic between seeing and knowing. The work bloody well offers you a new idea to see with, if you can see it, and in the midst of the tautologies and catch-22s implicit in that comment the spectator is born into the work or isn't. And much of the information comes through your body, like dance does (oddly enough, dancers want to dance in my work). Since it's not in the nature of good art to solicit the viewer like a tart on a street-corner, the work is to that degree engaged in a criticism (though that's too self-important a word) of the viewer or spectator or whatever we want to call the poor buggers invited to grade themselves in this pass/fail situation artists like me like to think of as moral test. It isn't of course, it's just another bit of evidence that most people don't pay attention—not just to your—or anyone else's—work, but to their own consciousness. But enough of this going on.

Camera (School of Visual Arts, 1975) for the first time correlated ropes and painted walls with several sightlines—places where the ropes captured floating zones of color on the wall. The sites of the four sightlines established a kind of conceptual rhomboid on the floor. For the first time, I learned how to mobilize walls and make them breathe, as it were. When framed within the ropes, and usually when seen with one eye (my work is full of one eye/two eyes questions, another sizable subject in itself) the colored areas floated out towards you,or— depending on the color—the reverse. I had wrestled another variable from the static box of a room and was ready to explore setting up those sets of reciprocal conditions that trap whatever content the work has. The next year in Todi, I demonstrated this idea to my own satisfaction by quietly encouraging a yellow rhomboid to become a square as one continuous, angled string lifted it gently off the wall. Bob Rauschenberg had been around to the studio and when looking at some work had said "Always a line man!" So I thought I'd show him.

Wall and floor—the usual limits of my activity—began to offer themselves more and more as questions rather than facts, and these questions were answered in two works (rope drawings #30 and #50) done two years apart. Number 30 was important for me since the serial ropes indicated two conclusions (see the drawing I've attached): the last—and lowest—

rope on the vertical side of the angle penetrated the floor (conceptually of course, just as two thirds of Robin's piece at Belfield is "under" the ground if the incised series are read correctly). And the top horizontal rope—if you read the series—penetrated the wall. So rather than being mobilized through framed zones of color, the limits of floor and wall were, with this piece, penetrated so that the idea of activity continuing *outside* the gallery, beyond and beneath, was introduced. I never went after the roof, except in the piece you saw at Nathan Kolodner's up the road (of course I always used it for attachments). All this—I see now—was part of similar concerns shared by a few others (Barry La Va really took this idea to the fair in a series of large drawings), but my penetrations were for another purpose.

In #50, the two ropes extending forward into the ground meet far under your feet, which has the effect of giving you a sense that the whole floor as you walk on it is a raised platform. So, in the simple-minded way that artists think, I felt I had raised the whole floor with minimal effort. The corridor thus formed as you stood directly in front of the work invited entry through the portal (a motif first introduced in *Camera* and much used by me since). And you walked into the darkness—and into the wall, which became a somewhat numinous power. Indeed the Vitruvian sense of stretching your hands and feet like the spokes of a wheel in my work is still a strong impulse for me. Just as the work (when you discover a sightline) pours itself into your eye (your eye becomes the vanishing point) so the spread-eagled body as you reach the other end of a sightline (when you can, that is) becomes the thing projected, the figure in the work, the place where one's body has its fullest consciousness. All this sounds pretty arcane, I suppose, but it's there.

The strongest expression of this raised floor idea was *Borromini's Underpass* (rope drawing #57)—Borromini being for me the prince of architects since he mobilizes space by the most sophisticated sightlines, curves, and spatial wrinkles, as well as see-sawing you between symmetry and asymmetry. I'm just nuts about him, since I feel I can hear him think. The *Underpass* is related of course to Borromini's famous little entertainment—the foreshortened tunnel in Rome, I forget exactly where. The placement of the ropes (see the drawing) was such that the figure walking the "raised" corridor appears suddenly to diminish or conversely, grow like a giant. And apart from watching, when you walked each direction yourself, you—or more truly your body—felt this too. So in this piece you easily became both watcher and watched, or, if you will, perceiver and perceived. This kind of split is a model of the serialized displacements I think—I hope—befalls the spectator in my work; they deposit other selves where they have been, and in my best pieces, there is a constant dialogue between the various phases of your former and subsequent selves as you increase and multiply . . .

In corners, space becomes a vortex, and I've had a lot to do with corners. Could I mobilize and cancel corners so that, just as I straightened out a labyrinth into a straight line in 1967/68, I could "straighten out" a room by eliminating its corners? I first eliminated a corner with several works that framed a yellow square in a corner, or really a compressed hexagon. The rather impressive climax of this idea was called *String Quartet* (Brooklyn Museum, 1982). As with *Borromini's Underpass* and *Red Room* (both done the same year, 1980) the entire room was painted a shade of gray, a twilight, a darkness that made the squares of color shine like windows. All four corners were described with one continuous string, the function of the string itself (apart from mobilizing the squares of color) being to articulate the space in which you walk.

In looking over the eleven-year history of rope drawings, I think these are some of the key works, along with *Kane* which you saw and wrote about in *The Times* (did you see Kenneth Baker's piece about it in *Art in America* last summer?). I think people missed one of the prime matters in that job—the relation of the movie screen to painting in, may I say pompously, the modernist period. *Kane,* of course, is Citizen Kane, and that work is quoted because it's the best American movie and has influenced everyone from here to Wajda. Is there one of our generation who hasn't sat enthralled by the granular, pearly potency of that magical rectangle before it is penetrated with shadows more real than our own lives? A considerable part of *Kane* was about that, as the furnace behind your back moved the red light steadily forward onto the "screen."

I suppose it's important to compare and contrast in a catalogue as to where the subject exposed on your dissecting table fits into the scheme of things. There are not too many installation workers left. Many have fled to paint and canvas. I suppose my friend Bob Irwin and Siah Armijani and George Trakis (all of whom I admire as colleagues) and Mary Miss who is a fine artist on another track, and yours truly are among the real survivors, (Judy Pfaff is one of the few recent artists to bring something new to installations—Miro-like submarine environments). As an old hand, I note that a few survive from each new venture—a half-dozen pop people, the first generation minimalists (Judd-Andre-Flavin), several among the second generation of minimalists (of whom I was one with LeWitt, Bochner, Eva Hesse, Peter Hutchinson, Smithson, and Dorothea Rockburne who is still a good friend, though you could say we were transitional in that we led into something else), one or two conceptualists, etc. My sixties' activities are gradually resurfacing as people drag them up, but the ropes—my main activity in the seventies—while they went to school in minimalism (as Edit Deak, I think, said)—are far from minimal in content. I suppose all this brings us, in my case, to the vexing question of impermanence, which must be tackled and I think you're well up on my thoughts on that (the obtuseness of objects and their egomaniacal chatter as they clutter the world, their graceless plunges towards history, their immodest groping towards the unborn, as if they were delivering posterity to themselves with high forceps. When all we have got and will ever have is *now*—one of three words, you may remember, that occupied—preoccupied—my sixties' drawings.)

This has gone on forever, and it's time I stopped. I hope it's some help to you, and feel free to use it or bend it to your own needs and words. So as they used to say in the country when I was a kid—more power to your elbow, and from the elbow down to the fingers on the typewriter.

Letter to Lucy Lippard
Critic, New York City
1985

It's I (me?) that's complimented that you are writing the NMAA catalogue intro. There's no one I would trust more. However, I suspect you don't take compliments well—no more than do I—so enough of that.

Since I've been a lousy curator of my past, I've had a bit of a time dragging things up. Like everyone else, I've lost a fair bit of stuff. Since the show goes back twenty years, I'm looking for—and finding—some early things, including the *Five Senses* drawings, which I hadn't seen for a long time. That was 65/66/67, and in 67 I got into the ogham drawings which have been with me one way or another since (the discipline, I mean, and the tendency to see things as language, including color as language). Thinking back to when we were all seeing each other, it was, for all the hysteria about turf, exhilarating. The future was out there like an open five-lane highway. Looking back, that particular highway had too many accidents. I remember a party at Bob Smithson's (when he mirrored the roof). I remember chatting with Eva, and we talked about Carl, who was on the other side of the room. She's long gone and so is Bob (and Andre's in bad trouble. I can't see any of this happening to color-field people; I don't think they live it the same way.)

I'm writing because I want to help out as best I can, traveling around in both our past selves. The *Five Senses* drawings reminded me of something basic to what I was doing: that the senses weren't just five inferior pathways to the citadel of ideas up there in the lighthouse, but were one and the same with it. You are what you see, touch, hear, feel, taste. My philosopher (and a strange philosopher he was) was, predictably, the old Bishop of Cloyne, Berkeley himself, who wrote some of the best aphorisms on perception I know. His was a splendid attack on material substance as something separate from the senses, with a large question mark delivered to "reality" out there, which is no more than a mirage through which we move to give it substance. I liked the idea that objects were no more than a group of fortuitous sensations that had agreed to cooperate in a way that would get you through the day (if they lied, you might, of course, get killed). Samuel Johnson's very English reaction to Berkeley was to kick a stone and say: "Thus I refute him!" I hope he hurt his bloody foot. I'm aware that good philosophy makes bad art; but the five senses, permuted and/or combined, gave me a lot of mileage insofar as idea and sensation are inseparable in a perception, and perception itself refutes the Carthesian split. We're all like fish in the same water, anyway, and the water is not very knowable. This is getting too grand, so let me get down to cases.

Berkeley, in effect, doubled your senses by making them both idea and sensation and object at once. So in one drawing I flattened the sensorium on a page (in magic squares so that anyway you sliced it, all the senses were in operation, but at different powers) so that you might plaster it on anything (like a poultice) and see (hear, etc.) what you would get. Then it was color-coded, then generated equations of objects that I hope have a bit of wit (or inwit) to them, then using the command (look, listen, touch, etc.) for each sense generated an omnibus word that had (would have) all the senses in it—which was then parsed and declined.

Since I think each of us mixes our senses differently, has different sense ratios, we each perceive a different world that we manage to agree upon enough to get our change right at the supermarket. Different cultures do this too, I think. So perception is the critical tissue through which the world knows us. So, you can understand my distaste for such terms as perceptual art, which is like calling Goya a "paint artist." It is not a category to be isolated while others get on with the strenuous business of dealing with content, with the real world and real issues. Nothing is more crucial than the way the mind and the senses interfuse to know themselves through—what? That's the question, and to me it was something absolutely concrete and absolutely abstract—number, repetition, color coding, gestalts, signs that fused language and idea in a minimal climate where you could see that old bum, ambiguity, flip-flop in slow motion.

I was never into the idea that the idea

makes the work, and we stand by, paring our nails. This works brilliantly for Sol. Or that the work can be made without the laying on of our hands, and this worked remarkably well for Judd and for Bob. I like the way Eva was always intellectually firm in her work no matter how "messy" some of it may have looked. I remember her saying "I hope you don't get too pure . . ." and there was no danger of that. Having the notion that the idea and the execution were inseparable, I wanted that familiar stranger, my own hand, on everything. Not because it was a special hand but because the early ogham drawings were about repetition, or number, or getting what was in the mind out there. I suppose there's certain primitive naiveté here. But in the execution, it is the effort after uniformity that measures the exact distance between head and hand, inside and outside, intention and object. The effort after the idea measures your own sensory pathways. And the senses become most interesting at the margins of their capacity. In this repetition, this effort after uniformity, there is divergence, irregularity, spacing inaccuracies, variations in height, degrees of pressure—none of which are sought. There is a sense of crisis to the degree that there is a threat of disorder which released could be overwhelming. I've always seen these drawings as stressful, as evidenced by false starts and lost temper. To witness the impulses along one's afferent and efferent nerves, the focusing of the eyes, the muscular tremors, is to watch that animal, hand, fidgeting in its conceptual cage.

There's more to say, I guess, but I think the hand thing is intrinsic to all the drawings, in the sense I mention it. It's not inconsistent with the impersonality of the work, which I shared with my friends, but on somewhat different terms. What sustained me then, and still does, is that the drawings had and have very little to do with me—the secular fellow reading the sports pages. But that's another idea, and I thought it might be useful, when I dug up some of the *Five Senses* drawings, to mention the sense of reality or unreality behind them. Nothing earth-shaking, but strongly felt. Art is artificial anyway, and those of us who stay close to it for a lifetime tend to become our art's artifact, an echo of its conventions. So before I dissolve into bodiless functions, I'll stop and go catch a plane to Washington.

Letter to Dominique Nahas
Curator, Everson Museum of Art, Syracuse, New York
July 4–5, 1987

Your letter mentioned that you would like some comments from me on the sixties' ogham sculptures. How hard that is for me to do now, twenty years later. But—let's give it a try. They were minimal in form, but that was the only minimal thing about them. Minimal objects were around from that mid-decade; I started these in 1967. They were, to my mind, clearly not minimal. Their form was determined by the need for an edge, a corner. It is around the corner that the ogham language inscribed itself on standing stones. So why not do them on any available corner? Why on reflective surfaces? Because I wanted to make their presence hallucinatory and ambiguous as they shuffled the reflected room (or gallery). Also inscribing lines on a reflective surface was like writing on water (remember Keats' great epitaph? "Here lies one whose name is writ on water"). Shift a step and the reflected room raced by while the inscribed line (done with a matt-knife) held firm. I'd used mirrors in boxes for much of the sixties. I should add, for the sake of period accuracy, that mirrors were an overused material in the sixties, carrying the dead weight of fashion, which hampered my use of them. By 1967 they were going out of fashion and so became all-the-more usable for me. I'd explored mirroring in a series of photographs done in 1967. Also, funny though it sounds, I'd learned a lot from photographing the Las Vegas signs, which embody in a highly sophisticated way matters of symmetry and asymmetry. These photographs were reproduced in *Art in America* in 1973.

Mirrors are both surface and depth and what and how they reflect, including yourself, is a rich subject. In there is the Through the Looking Glass space, and some great artworks have been done in mirroring, including marvelous performances by Chaplin and Fred Astaire as they mimic their mirrored image, which turns out to be someone else. So there was a fictive space, reflecting a world alternatively paralyzed or in motion depending on the spectator, who became intrinsic whether she or he liked it or not. Of course, if you're still and other things are moving, the space in the mirror is restless. The idea was to make the fact of reflecting as much a *fact* as possible, indeed a fact before-the-fact, if I can say that—since mirroring was casual and unconsidered in most of the works I saw. Not much thought about the nature of reflections (no reflection on reflection!).

The structures evolved—the "canvas" as it were—were basically corners in several configurations from which I rarely departed. They were Vs (positive and negative) and Ws. The Vs could come out from the wall thus (in plan); or they could be inverted, thus:

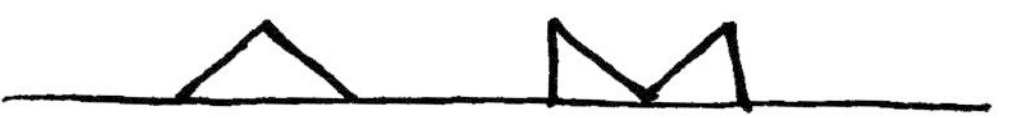

You could put two corners together, then get a rectangle.

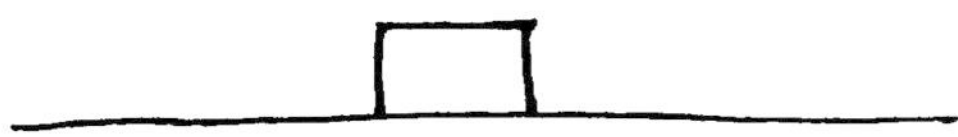

Or you could put positive and negative Vs together and get a W with wings, a "flying W," thus:

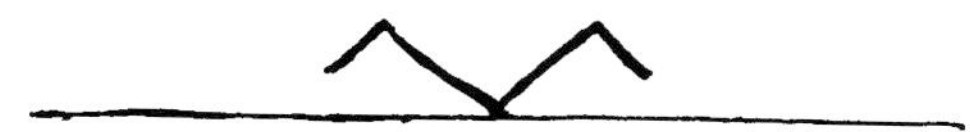

Each of these disposed the surroundings (including the spectator) differently. The positive or averted Vs, split him/her, like the prow of a ship, gathering in a 90-degree arc of the environment while leaving a 45-degree "dead" or silent zone for the frontal spectator. I always fancied this as a kind of mute explosion, abutting widely separated strips of the surroundings. The inscribed lines (scratched or etched into the soft aluminum) had their own way of taking the light—quietly going white or dark depending on how the work was lighted. The top of the columns usually were full of light (sometimes they seemed white-hot), while the lower parts were generally dark, except for the light *in* the lines.

In the inverted Vs, with the two strips of polished aluminum at angles of 90 degrees (and sometimes, purposely a little more or less), the reflected space exactly replicated the space in the room because *it was not a mirror image*. The optics of this are simple enough. At 90 degrees, two mirrors reflect their reflections, and thus no longer rotate your image. The space you're standing in and the space inside—the doubly reflected space—are continuous with one another. You could shake hands with yourself in the doubled mirror, or see your face as it is to others. Indeed you could walk parallel to the wall and pass your own image going in the other direction. Thus one had canceled the basic illusion of mirroring by means of a double illusion (two reflections). Again, you had a sophisticated canvas on which to inscribe lines and language.

With the Ws, you had both a doubly and singly reflected space composed of positive and negative Vs. Again, it seemed to me, a sensitive "canvas" on which to work. You had a concertinalike effect on the environment—the outside wings thrown out to the environment, the narrow central "doorway" continuing the space in which you stand, with some strips of space outside it crossing up the environment. Hard to follow, but in terms of optics, rather neat. In the minimal era, such structures would have been read as minimal objects. They were however, just canvases for me, waiting for the language that would articulate their shape and structure, making literal and conceptual connections to the mirroring itself. I was far along a lonely road, but of that, at the time, I had no notion.

And what of the lines inscribed on this slippery surface? Or rather, the language? After spoken language came the rigorous mysteries of shape and grammar. The shapes of all languages are as arbitrary as a butterfly's flight, yet groups and communities and peoples share this arbitrariness. The wonders of language are quickly lost; words are used to conceal themselves, to lie as much as to instruct, to blur as much as to communicate. Language's "skeleton," then, can be fleshed out with as many varieties of moral and other ambiguities as there are people. And language in art? Yet another universe where language—words, letters—are given another forked tongue, doing double duty in a foreign place. It was my fancy that language—treacherous though it was—could be splinted, held, mirrored, and unmirrored in unambiguous splendor. Or at least some words could. To this end I did structural plays, which "rotated" sentences through several possible meanings, each very firmly held. Several "voice-works" (I guess you'd call them) sounded out the same idea, and sometimes reversed it (made something very simple virtually indecipherable).

All this is conventional enough. But how to do it in sculpture? I wanted to get rid of the Roman alphabet's nonsensical shapes. These shapes, as we know, have as much relation to sound as words have to the object they describe. At the time, the isolation which language breaks and then frequently restores through its usage was much with me (at that time I did a sort of treatise on language—and on some other things—in a publication called *Aspen 5/6*). Since that time, so much has been done on language that we often seem to be no more than language's puppets, lapsing into sawdust as the bubble of language is passed from lip to lip. What lives is this bubble, this convention, the artifact, the fragile agreement. What dies is the tongue that speaks it. Where could I find a language that had sufficient logic that thinking could decipher it? Thoughts of music were not far away.

I searched for a language that would have an intrinsic logic, a sign system that eliminated shapes. I searched in precolumbian languages and calendars, studied how hieroglyphs gradually abstracted stick figures and symbols (hieroglyphs reek with their origins), ran through Scandinavian runes, Greek alphabets (very tick-tack), Chinese and Japanese (even more staccato), elegant Farsi, looking for my Rosetta stone. Then, like the purloined letter, there is was in my own backyard all the time. I'd known ogham as a kid in school and back it came in one exultant rush. Here was the purest sign system ever devised, clean as a whistle, as logical in its four registers as the four sets of serial music. Gone were the curlicues and ticks of Rome; here instead were the short clean lines of a logical delight. And all that articulated the language was—a corner, an edge, a line across which you read—the horizon of language suddenly found! I still feel that exhilaration. Ogham moved my work, became its primum mobile, for many a year.

What was ogham? (I had to answer that a thousand times to uncomprehending faces). It's a translation of twenty letters of the Roman alphabet into lines. Two are superfluous—Q and Z, which don't exit in Gaelic. Why such redundancy? Beats me. Anyway, all you need in any language is the vowels, and enough consonants to take them for a walk. Here's the way they go:

H P T C Q B L V S N

A O U E I M G Ng Z R

This is classical ogham, simple and to the point—or line. The Irish, who could never leave anything alone, embellished this basic system in wonderfully imaginative ways, which are summarized in *The Book of Ballymote*. But this relapse back into shapes was to be avoided. At last, I had my linear language, the purest sign system ever devised, returning a faint echo from fifteen hundred years back, but for all practical purposes (except mine) buried in silence. A dead language? Yes, but what a language. It spoke to the idea of language, to serial music and to minimalism's reductive paradox. It would have been different had I devised a language myself. That was modernism's habit, but everyone turned out to be speaking modernism, which was socialized as a compendium of styles. It was to be cherished that my language wasn't mine, and dead to boot. It was thus true artifact, as all language is, with the paradoxes of speaker and what is spoken (does the language die as we speak it, or are we language's corpse?). Also, you could communicate through this language by knocks and taps alone—a kind of rudimentary serial music? At this time, Morton Feldman and I were inseparable. Sol, by the way, was very much into serialism. I introduced Morty to him and to another of his admirers, Eva Hess. Eva may have been the most original artist I ever met. I also did some choruses at this time, which of course I didn't show to Morty. His idea of indeterminacy was at odds with serialism's (and indeed minimalism's) strict rulebook.

But back to the crucial edge. The vertical edge articulates the language of across, right, and left. Or if you make the edge horizontal (which I did particularly in the drawings) across, above, and below. You can still read ogham on standing stones in Ireland and parts of Scotland. What was it used for? To establish ownership, mark boundaries, and for commemorative purposes. No trivia, like the great Mesopotamian word lists. You didn't hack at the stone in whimsy. It wasn't for making proclamations. Just a name, a border, a memorial: the standing stone, speaking through its edges. Ogham made for easy reading; a blind man could read it with his fingers. Early Irish art was about line, always line. But why the Irish Celts chose to turn language into line is a mystery to me. During the Celtic revival of course, the mystery was amplified. The language would change, by the way, depending on whether you read it up or down. (A little tilt of the head there.)

The vowels are particularly beautiful: A-O-U-E-I in one to five strokes across the edge or line. There is strict segregation of the vowels in Gaelic. The broad vowels (A-O-U) and the slender (E-I) must behave according to the etiquette which is never relaxed. Take the word now—"anois." It's pronounced an-ish, with a slight accent on the second syllable. You don't sound the "o." So why is it there? Because on either side of a consonant, you *must* be broad or slender. In Gaelic this is called "caol le caol agus leathan le leathan"—broad to broad and slender to slender. Broad and slender vowels can kiss, snuggle, or bump as much as they like when the consonantal duenna is out of the way—as in "aon" (one), or "bean" (woman). I did many works on the vowels alone, including sound works and the performance "Vowel Grid" (of which I'm enclosing a photograph). Of all my immediate colleagues at that time, the only one similarly fascinated with language was Dan Graham.

So now I had my reflective "canvas" and my language. A language that was serial in form and so could be composed as well as written. There were ghosts of seriality in ogham—there was the set, one over the set, one under the set, but without the reversals. And of course serialism was in our mother's milk in the mid and late sixties. It was a way of reading art rather than recognizing compositions. Serialism and sets made for busy reading. It's a mode of perception that's gone now—the young see differently—but it made the eye a gymnast, with some of the gymnast's leaps and thrills. I suppose each art has a mode of perception buried in it, and the future brings foreign eyes—eyes that don't speak the language, as it were.

Now a whole linguistic universe lay open to me. I had a new mouth but what was I to utter? There was no hesitation about this for me. I had a somewhat primitive sense of words as objects, augmented when repetition numbs the meaning out of the sound, leaving what Stuart Davis might call a sound-shape. What do you think are the most important words (or concepts) in the language, if you were limited to a few? Mine were predominantly three: One, Here, and Now. Easy to see why. One dealt with indivisibility, any form of absolutism that disappears when you say Two. That oneness also encompassed the spectator (and sometimes their reflected image. It also signified the indivisibility of the word itself and its "body," the linear signs that carried it, and in turn the structure that carried those lines. The first works were frequently made up of several columns, but I quickly limited myself to one. A lot to get into one thing. So it was a peculiar kind of absolutism really, one reflected in the permutations of one which became the substance of a key work (Lucy Lippard has the first drawing for it).

Here and *Now* intersect as they do as this moment, and as they did in several drawings. But I usually separated them in the sculptures, where they shared a key notion. Several *heres* or several *nows* can only be seen one at a time. Thus all the other *heres* became theres, and all the other *nows* became either future or past—because you can't see more than one thing at the same time. But if there were several *heres* or *nows*, how were they positioned and what did that position do to your perception of them? The plot thickened. Even more so when the words were reflected, and reflected again. So the perception of the word or words was far from its image on a printed page, or from concrete poetry which, brilliant though it can sometimes be, doesn't convince me spatially very often; and reading tends quickly to take the content out of its words. The majesty of the word, it seems to me, is a far more serious matter, much though I appreciate all forms of play.

I'm skipping over a great deal and limiting myself to the primary words. (Zero—making something out of nothing—I used occasionally, but you had to be careful with zero). There was a lot of other (usually) one-shot things: the idea of language (e.g. six ones in six languages), the notion of encoding and decoding, the paradoxes of literal and visual language, hermeticism and communication, placement and displacement, (placement as language), objecthood versus dematerialization, the absent work/the doubly present spectator (as the works slipped into a maze of reflections), jokes (of course)—indeed (I thought modestly) speculations on the nature of art and its odd history as language, serialism, and minimalism were fused into a single idea in works that I was convinced were an invention, and to that degree ungenerous to whatever predecessors might be invented for them. They abandoned literalism, and classic minimalism's cul-de-sac, becoming—as their words fused into substance—mildly iconic. And all of this, I hope, very gently done through a kind of whispering. Whispering, after all, gets full attention!

The articulation of the reflections was very carefully thought out. Take a *one*. In the Vs and Ws the *one* will be reflected in the space within, the reverse or mirrored V (which is, you remember, continuous with your own space since it is not a mirror image. Your *other* self (mirrored within) can "see" this mirrored ONE also. So both of you, you and your image can see the same thing from opposite sides, thereby raising a question of where (who) you are. Placement as identity overlaps and slips off the elusive self. I could also vary your image within by slightly opening or closing the 90-degree angle between the two strips of polished aluminum. Sometimes, I chose to eliminate your image altogether (by slightly opening the 90-degree V). Then you looked in the mirror and saw no reflection.

There were six possible reflections, exploiting fully the symmetries and asymmetries intrinsic to mirroring. Just as the Vs and Ws developed an X-effect—that is four Vs touching at their points—you have four types of corners across which ogham could be read. One is the actual V and its scratches; the other is the totally reflected V within; each of the two others are composed of one actual and one reflected strip (the lateral reflections; I'll leave you to spot the asymmetries (that is the asymmetrical "reflections" which can be read in the N).

Finally, there is the dialogue between the scratched lines and the mirroring. The lines themselves could be made (up and down) symmetrical and nonsymmetrical. Here interval, regularity, repetition, etc. were brought into play. So there was a farther conceptual territory to be staked out between the literal (the scratched lines) and the reflected. And having mobilized mirroring into asymmetries as well as symmetries, I had a vocabulary that could have kept me going indefinitely.

The works were, of course, met with puzzlement, wariness, and little commentary. The word went around to unwary writers: "There's some kind of language in there, so watch out." Yet this was a time when intellectual rigor was prized, and several writers (Lucy particularly) could follow you anywhere. I greatly overestimated the audience's perceptiveness and tenacity and, in what I view now as culpable innocence, didn't realize that what was seen by several as the beauty of the work (a side-product—I didn't show the "too beautiful" ones) forestalled penetration. I was asking for a great deal, I suppose—nothing less than a community of sorts in which communion rather than communication was my desire. But intention is a poor pilot, and the works seemed further sealed as time went by. But like Christy Mahon's daddy, up they arise again, to my puzzlement and pleasure. There has been more interest in them over the past few years than at any time since they were made, and they are passing that acid capitalist test—being bought. Poor sculptures—I'm sure much incomprehension lies ahead for them. *Caveat emptor*. Time, however, seems to have a persistent low-grade IQ. As the works drink up time, people seem to get them better. I've gone on immoderately, but that is a function of who you are writing to. When I sat down, there was little expectation that the door of memory would open, but it turned out to be a revolving one. If this overlong letter is helpful, it's accomplished its aim. There's always more to say, but enough's enough!

Letter to Rainer Crone and David Moos
Critics, New York City
October 14, 1990

I'd like to follow up the *Big H* material sent from Belfast with some background to the politics of the unpleasantness in the North of Ireland. The photographs of the excremental cells are particularly moving, I think. There are also some aerial shots of the H-Block prison (I'll have to find out its official name). Need I say I'm delighted the two of you are examining this work— which you both journeyed to Belfast to see—since it is close to my heart for several reasons, not least that it was done by an identity formulated in response to the Derry massacre in 1972, when the British army shot down thirteen unarmed people on yet another Bloody Sunday. The British, by the way, insist that Derry be called Londonderry, part of the linguistic violence inflicted on the "natives" during the repression of Gaelic speech.

The conflict in Northern Ireland is enigmatic to virtually everyone I meet, and they plaintively ask if a solution is possible. Americans hate to think there are no solutions to problems, part of an idealism inherent in the American character, I guess. But there's no solution I can see to the blue-collar war intermittently killing and maiming thousands since it began in 1969. I was in the north with Barbara in 1969, just before it all started, and you could smell the coming violence, just as you can go to some southern cities and towns here and smell the hatred. History lies heavy across the entire island, nowhere more smotheringly than in the north. The remote origins of the conflict are ever-present. In the seventeenth century, in a massive program of social engineering, the English confiscated hundreds of thousands of acres in the north, after the Cromwellian repression (Cromwell went through Ireland like Grant through the South), and imported tens of thousands of lowland Scots to settle the land. The natives were driven, in a famous phrase "to hell or to Connaught"—Connaught being a stony western province unable to support much life. The settlers were Protestant and loyal to the Crown. The displaced natives were Catholic, loyal to Rome, and rebellious. The two cultures have bred out pretty much as expected, though some of the subsequent rebellions were led by leaders of Scottish-Irish derivation (remember there's no such thing as a "Scotch" person; all you can do with Scotch is drink it). The Scots-Irish stock has been generous to this country, giving it several presidents (including Richard M. Nixon) and millionaires (the Mellons). But why, you may ask, is there a Northern Ireland at all, since Ireland succeeded in its final rebellion against England and became the Irish Free State in 1922?

It's an old story now, and you see it rehearsed everywhere. The Sikhs want a part of India, just as Pakistan took its big bite when the British left. The Basques want part of Spain. Tribal minorities in Africa want territory and nationhood. The Protestant majority in the north refused to join the new Free State and Lloyd George, the British prime minister, promised "immediate and terrible war" if the Irish delegation in London refused to accept the secession of the six northern counties from the new Free State. The delegation agreed, went back, failed to sell the compromise to the rest of the revolutionaries; thus the short, vicious Irish civil war. In these events, my mother's side of the family (Brennans) was active, being killers or heroes, depending on your politics.

So Northern Ireland, a quasi-country with its own parliament (at Stormont), was invented as part of the United Kingdom. The majority: a million Protestant Scots-Irish; the minority: a half million Catholics. The Orange and the Green. These two colors bear a heavy symbolic cargo that goes back to the seventeenth century, when a battle of European importance was played out on Irish soil. In the Battle of the Boyne, which much of Europe watched anxiously, Protestant William of Orange defeated Catholic King James and his French and Irish allies on the 12th of July, 1690, thus preserving the British throne for the Protestant faith. Every 12th, the Orangemen parade in Belfast to commemorate their salvation from the dominance of Rome. The Pope is taken very personally by the Orange north, much as Americans used to see the Ayatollah Khomeni. The Green, in contrast, is part of the lore of Irish nationalism, and "The Wearing of the Green" (as one popular song puts it) has traditionally been the insignia of protest and rebellion.

Why the present low-grade civil war in the north? Isn't the province better off than the Catholic republic to the south, with better social services, better roads, higher incomes, and massive British subsidy? All true. But the majority in the north, fearful of what they perceive as a voracious Catholic majority down south, ingeniously deny their Catholic minority their civil rights. Voting districts are altered to favor the election of Protestants ("gerrymandering," a word like "boycott," generated by Irish repression); housing and jobs are denied Catholics. So added to the religious (Protestant/Catholic), and national (loyalists versus republicans), antipathies is the third member of this ugly trinity, economics. Hence the violence, hence the hunger strikes, hence the terrorist Irish Republican Army, and the terrorist Urban Defence League—the IRA and the UDF. This is the background against which *Big H* was done—a matrix of injustice, religious intolerance, nationalistic hatreds generating the usual paranoias, violence, and fear.

The work had a very precise vibration in its context. Falls Road (the Catholic area regularly swept by the tanks and half-tracks of the occupying army) was a few blocks away. The H-Block itself, where the political prisoners are detained, is a few miles as the crow flies. According to current law, suspected persons can be held and detained without trial; the H-Block has its own ugly history of mistreatment (Amnesty International reports). There has been a long argument in the north about the taxonomy of protest. Are you a criminal or a political prisoner? The IRA (like the PLO, a terrorist organization with a political wing, Sinn Fein) claims political status for its arrested members. Mrs. Thatcher, in the 1980s, denied that status. The prisoners, refusing to wear the uniform of the common criminal, were confined to their cells without services, in their accumulating excrement. In protest, the prisoners smeared the walls of their cells with their shit.

This extraordinary gesture, which would surely have interested Norman O. Brown, is the source of the scumbled browns of *Big H*. The "dirty protest," as it was called, struck deep with me. Its aims were clear: to expose the deprivations imposed on the prisoners by degrading the degradations they were experiencing, making a positive protest out of these two negatives; to give their corporeal selves a context generated from within their own bodies, to that degree appropriating the very structure that confined them; to transgress the taboos associated with the body's wastes by using that waste as a wordless but powerful rhetoric, thereby giving the British phrase the "dirty Irish" a literal meaning and a reverse spin; and, of course, to win back political status by soliciting public outrage. The attempt failed, but the thought of these young men, also called the blanket men, since they wrapped themselves in their blankets rather than wear prison uniform, crouching in their cells, incarcerated within walls painted with their shit, is heartbreaking—however misguided their extremism, an extremism, it should be noted, provoked by the complete failure of political process.

These then were the components of *Big H*: an orange H in a pyramid of green, two dismally dissonant colors, surrounded by the dirty protest, and further bracketed by a massive, dark split H, its crossbar running (conceptually) behind the entire work. The "H," the pyramid, and the painted "door" were framed and concentrated by the string when you stood at the perspective point, which I call the vanishing point, for the entire work at that place rushes into the eye and is thrown back—projected—with one's stare. There's a great exchange of energy here, I believe. At the vanishing point for *Big H* all the wheeling parallaxes paused to frame a bilateral symmetry that echoed the observer's body. Sighting with one eye, you are deprived of the stereoscopic vision that helps you stand firmly. So matters of balance come into play as the sightline is found—and lost with the slightest movement. The work—string and painted wall—is implicated in the feedback between the eye and the body's kinesthesias. People "choreograph" themselves at this point, as the body delivers its checks and balances to their stance. It is at that point also that their ideas may be rearranged. On the floor of the *Big H* gallery, at the viewer's feet, was painted a small orange "H."

I was careful that the work had enough neutrality to provoke both sides in different ways. The Loyalists could see a powerful orange "H" blazoned on a field of green, asserting itself over that pestilential color and the surrounding shit. The Republicans could see the hated "H" about to be engulfed by the rising pyramid of noble green, eventually opening the prison door held between the lower limbs of the H, a generative position surely. (Though I abhor Freud, there was some dark humor here.) The intellectuals deciphered this easily enough; some refused to enter the gallery on hearing about the work's political nature. The review in *Circa* (enclosed with the Belfast material) remained temperate until rising anger spilled over, based in part on the "outsider" charge. What right had I to comment on the residents' pain when I did not share it with them every day? As if we must hold our tongues at any injustice whether in the Gaza Strip or Kuwait.

I had some of the same response to my name-change in 1972. This was certified in a performance before thirty witnesses and a notary, at a Dublin space, assisted by two radical artists. The theme of this change was language (a structural play), color (the orange and the green), and a simulated atrocity (there are photographs of this). The change of name is accepted now, but at the time it annoyed many of my compatriots at home. I can understand that. Who was I to take on the name of my country? It would be an arrogant gesture surely, were I not an expatriate whose career was abroad. One formidable woman artist insisted that Ireland was by gender female, not male—true enough, since in the literature of protest, Ireland is often seen as a homeless old woman; by usurping her, my phantom cock was poised between rape and incest. I undertook to sign my work "Patrick Ireland" until the occupying army left Northern Ireland and civil rights were restored. My friends responded in various ways. Rudolf Baranik, whom I didn't know then, called me up to endorse the gesture. Lee Krasner said, "You'll be Patrick Ireland forever." My dealer at the time, Betty Parsons, wasn't too pleased. A name-change (I discovered) involves serious adjustments internally and externally. To the degree that you are an object you are renamed, as if a kettle were hereafter to be known as a telephone. The name was carefully chosen. Ireland is the last thing Brits want to hear about. And young Irish farm boys trying to make a living in London are called, with condescension, "Paddys." I was determined to make Patrick Ireland a name of some dignity and substance. Since all my work after 1972 has been made by "Patrick Ireland," who was born out of injustice, every work, no matter what its other content, is to that degree political.

What relationship has all this to the *Inverted Pyramid for Cyclops* at Cowles—apart from the common pyramid, which I've used in several rope drawings and early sculptures? The aims were very different indeed, but both involved architecture, and the matter of location, of inside/outside. I've been painting whole rooms since 1980, delivering their neutral space into place as best I can. The rooms always include the figure in the space, the spectator who is generally ignored in architecture and who, through various placements of ropes and walls is nudged, seduced, invited but never coerced into taking a walk, much as the eighteenth century construed walking, with prospects, the view of the landscape, near and far, changing with the slow incremental rhythms of perambulation. Indeed, the labyrinth in the next room at Cowles was generated in part from my interest (in the sixties) in formal gardens and the experience of passing through those rectangles, arcs, and lozenges in which nature was encouraged to conform to a geometric order which enhanced it.

Since this spectator was intrinsic to each work, I thought a lot about him/her and learned how to endow a position or place with magnetism or its opposite, making vistas and pathways, viewpoints and look-outs (and look-ins) where the curious spectators (curiosity being a great ally) would find their body taking them. Oddly enough, my best audiences are in San Francisco and Germany; in New York, the spectators tend to look *at* the work rather than find themselves in it. The frustration this sometimes provokes is the closest I get to modernist rage at the spectator.

I think you have something I wrote for an architectural magazine about how a single spectator populates a space with his/her future and past perambulations and so becomes his/her own multitude. Also how watching another person in the space partakes of that. And what kind of experience that is. Like any area of discourse, this can be pushed to the extremes of complete freedom (meaningless) and complete coercion (frightening), each of which has, of course, its political analogue. Insofar as the work implicates or suggests or develops a way of behavior, it raises the question of what kind of behavior occurs in the work, which is in the gallery, which is in the building, which is in the street, which is in the city, which is part of the culture? (I'm trying to say the gallery is a social construct, and the work has a social coefficient within that construct, towards which it has an attitude.)

Like every building we occupy or pass through, every installation involves matters of control, movement, usage, hierarchies of space, habit, diverse function; it deals with entrances and exits, encounters and avoidance, the individual and the crowd. There is a missing history of behavior in modernism, not just before paintings where the options are near and far, but in so-called environmental works, from Mondrian, Tatlin, Duchamp, etc. on. The spectator, the poor soul now stunned with reception esthetics, is too often absent in our histories of modernist art, architecture, and to some extent, theater. Modernism frequently punished the spectator; the price of enlightenment (or admission) was abuse. To punish the spectator now is, it seems to me, to continue the tactics of a war long over.

The spectator's response in my case can be forestalled with such notions as "perception" and a brand name like "perceptual art." To call my stuff "perceptual art" is as silly as calling, say, Franz Kline "a paint-and-canvas artist." The notion of "perceptual art" comes, I suppose, from the employment of the eye's physiology in ways that dwell upon its abilities to resolve and generate spatial conundrums, just as the brief half-life of op art in the sixties was based on the psychology textbook. The result was, I believe, to detain visual data in a kind of perceptual loop that, like basic psychology diagrams, is simultaneously fascinating and boring. (Although you can make art out of anything, including this "perceptual" swamp; Bridget Reilly did). I think what a knowledge of visual perception does for an artist (it certainly does for me) is to provide a vocabulary, and how you employ that vocabulary is not too different from asking a writer what he or she does with those artificial, socially endorsed and socially limited constructs called words. I see perceptual sophistication as its own spatial avenue to poetry, and poetry has its own metaphors, images, similes, epigrams, displacements of meaning, mysterious contiguities, renovations of cliches, planned redundancies, rhymes, and rhythms, beats and off-beats, ironies, wit, and fierce pleasures. Can all that be transferred to space? You're damn right it can.

But that's only a part of the story. Poetic insight or outsight, or whatever, takes you only so far. And, indeed, "poetry" applied to visual art connotes a kind of issueless self-indulgence. What I'm talking about is the hard *poetics* of the visual, an area hardly scratched in art-writing. But to return to the abandoned spectator, who has been left wandering in a presumptive rope drawing. The question that follows is: what is your view of that exalted and disastrous anima that we all are? Maybe each artist's work answers that question in terms of a precisely achieved set of moods.

"My" spectator, if I can use the possessive, is a secular figure, moving through chromatic parallaxes and vistas where, at each new place, his/her arrival has been anticipated, until every inch of the space has been charged by his/her passage and by his/her gaze as it sprays out in the staccato rhythms of noticing: check the floor (where am I?); follow lines to their points of attachment including the ceiling (the space that contains me); replace what you see through the involuntary eclipses of blinks (our built-in slide machine); abandon stereoscopic safety to "put on" a sightline, frame the painted wall with rope, so that you can move an entire wall towards you by merely closing an eye (the classic esthetics of push/pull); watch others as they become your proxies, your spectacles; all the time rehearsing and anticipating, creating the space through which you walk by marking its wilderness with the unmistakable signature of your occupancy. I watch spectators in rope drawings choreograph themselves as they focus a sightline, often as if they were unused to putting their bodies to work. Dancers, who occupy their bodies as easily as they occupy a space, always seem to get my work. Locating a sightline keeps your body busy sending a stream of information up to your eye and back down again; to some degree your eye becomes your body and your body your eye, *except* there are brief moments of perfect focus when the body drops away and you become an eye, a glimpse not only of the artwork, but often of an axial symmetry that echoes that of the (temporarily) departed body. The spectator is always free to decline (I regret I cannot be present) the implicit invitation of these ropes drawings. Many do. But then, I believe most people are not present to themselves and do not pay much attention to anything, including themselves. Dancers do, kids do, the so-called unlettered frequently do, as do some of the sophisticated. As time has gone by, however, I realize I ask more of the audience than I thought I did when I began years ago.

All this is process, spectator's process. But what is the spectator looking at? In most of my recent work lines in space are projected from chosen points onto the walls which are then painted. The lines generally add up to a structure, whether "house" or "pyramid" or "corridor." There is an inside (the rope structure) and an outside (between the structure and the pained walls). But since the walls of the structure (defined by the lines of rope) are projected on to the actual walls, you can be outside the inside but inside the outside, i.e., in a space that is inhabited by several concepts, depending on which set of cues you take your bearings from. In fact, you can be inside and outside at the same time. When inside the rope pyramid at Cowles you were outside the projected pyramids on the walls, and when outside the pyramid of ropes, you were also outside the projected walls (though obviously in the gallery!): thus you were doubly "outside" and, if two negatives make a positive, you were cancelled into a presence. . . .

People get this in their own ways. I remember Louis le Brocquy saying, "I felt like a ghost, passing through the walls of the transparent house." Leslie Katz said of another piece, "I've never been *inside* a drawing before." What I'm after in several recent pieces, including the pyramid—and Mike Brenson's comments got this—is a kind of architectural deconstruction (not in a poststructuralist sense, more in the hard-hat sense) that reinterprets the notion of domestic (house) and public (pyramid) structures, which are, of course, laden with wonderful baggage which I can profitably inflect. Each wall of *Inverted Pyramid for Cyclops* varied in mood, scale, and content. If you read counter-clockwise, it went from tomb (an optimistic tomb with the light coming from within), to harsh desert, to massive skewed wedge (showing three sides of a four-sided pyramid) to a gentle exit in twilight through a blue door (said Lucy Lippard: "I want to go through the blue door").

Intrinsic to this subject are of course the primal entities of window, door, wall, portal, arch, as well as a history or architecture you can summon with a shape; also intrinsic is (back to him/her again) the spectator who is (I believe) ignored and often insulted by architects. Yet architects are empowered to determine our relationships in the curious medium through which we swim, glide, and stagger. I deeply believe (who doesn't?) that every artificial space inflects our behavior. We know that space has its economics; it also has its politics and gender. I ask of every architect's building, where is the occupant? In the international style, the occupant was simply missing—not even a poor Polonius lurking behind the curtain (wall); in recent architecture, there is often an encouraging sense of play, though some buildings seem to solicit the presence of mutants and ciphers. We are all aware of the repressive nature of most public and corporate structures; CBS's Black Rock on Sixth Avenue is a perfect dark cover for the betrayals and assassinations that occur within. My favorite is the FBI building in Washington; a likely fortress for the secret police, squatting on Pennsylvania Avenue with the density of a black hole.

My question (to myself) is: "Can I construct a temporary place in which spectators may find themselves in a structure which empowers that search?" It's not always a happy experience. Some rooms had their own harsh set of references (e.g., *Big H, Borromini's Underpass*). I suppose it depends on your thoughts, your mood when you're doing it, and recently (thank Heaven) it's been (I don't know why) one of exhilaration and blessed delight.

Even the labyrinth from 1967 in the last show, though its mood was weighty, was far from gloomy. Its enclosure never threatened; it left numerous exits as it spun its spokes from the center, and encouraged an easy transit (the classic purification) or dawdling and surprise. It had its moods. People meeting each other within seemed to share some implicit contract that overcame the forced intimacies of encounter with a smile; a group of (multicultural) kids disappeared within and set the place echoing with laughter. So I guess it was a smiling labyrinth for all its solemnity. To my surprise, its spectator had great deal in common with the spectator in the rope drawings. For me the minimal adventure, which I shared with my colleagues back in the sixties, made things richer rather than poorer, and opened up almost symphonic possibilities with just a few notes. There were some who held to the ideology of minimalism as a monk to his crucifix. But while I loved the discipline, I didn't have the (American?) habit of institutionalizing it in one's psyche, no matter how brilliant the results. I think minimalism was far more important than any "movement" since abstract expressionism. But I doubt if you'll ever sell that notion to history, which misinterprets the minimal idea consistently. Have you read Kenneth Baker's book? It's splendid and should help recover the primary impulse behind what used to be called primary structures. Lucy Lippard's work here is, as usual, indispensable. But I'm getting away from rope drawings, and I've certainly gone the long way around on what I thought would be a short journey.

I hope all this stuff helps somewhat, and I thank you both for your interest in my work. I'm aware of how pretentious writing about your own things can be, so I've done my best to avoid the chronic egomania endemic to my trade. With luck I'll be able to read this again sometime in the future without a blush. . . .

Letter to William Lieberman
Curator of Twentieth-century Art, Metropolitan Museum of Art, New York
October 20, 1990

I hasten to answer your questions about the "stone" drawing you acquired for the Met.

It was one of a series done, as far as I remember, in 1982/83 arising out of visits to pre-Celtic and Celtic sites in Ireland, made in 1975 and 1978—the latter when doing an hour on "The Treasures of Ireland" show at the Met for CBS. Why the delay? I kept thinking about them—the stones—until I had to get them out of my head.

The great tombs in the Boyne Valley at New Grange, north of Dublin, are as powerful as anything I've seen. They date from 3000 B.C. to 1500 B.C., depending on who's doing the dating. Nothing is known about the builders. They knew enough to coax the equinoctial sun through a slit in the entrance, through a passage, into the vaulted burial chamber within. What kind of society (hunting, agriculture) generated these tombs? No one knows. But like the Celts after them (the Celts came to Ireland late, around the first century A.D.), they invoked the spiral as their most intimate signature. Incised on boulders in a kind of dogged fever, repeated, reversed and repeated again in changes of scale and direction, following contours in and out, as if the rock were breathing, it is a form, I guess, animating the stones, giving them a spirit that in some way guides the spirits within on their voyage, as well as magically protecting the tomb.

Well, maybe—who knows? But the great capstones to those tombs in Brittany and Ireland are crawling with patterns that must have had some significance other than decoration. It's just too hard on the hands to groove and pit and chip the stone from a decorative impulse alone. So in making those drawings I had a sense of rehearsing the stones' original function as I construed them, (thus that halting, biting, hatchet-line

line), and a sense of tattooing a living surface, though the surface at hand was only the usual acid-free paper. I did this while trying to avoid romanticizing remote prehistory, which was unquestionably brutal.

I was just sending a modest, transmillennial greeting card to some vanished ancestors. Speaking of messages, I had, since the sixties, borrowed from the old Irish standing stones the ogham alphabet with its perfect serial system, for my aluminum sculptures which, in the way of the world, drew only a few but passionate followers then, and which over the past few years have been happily resurrected.

I stopped the stone drawings after doing about fifteen or twenty. But they had their effect on the painted rooms I did later, gave them more depth and atmosphere, I think, as I began to think more clearly about architecture, and those matters of inside and outside that have preoccupied me since them.

I am delighted the stone is at the Met through your good offices. Nothing could give me greater pleasure than to have it shown at the Met, where I wandered in awe on my first visit to this country in 1956.

Letter to Carter Ratcliff
Critic, New York City
April 27, 1991

I'm enclosing two bits and pieces: one, something I wrote on installations for *Architectural Digest*; the other, a catalogue of early rope drawings from a touring show, with a marvelous mad article by Edit Deak. I hope they engage your interest, by which, I should add, I am much complimented.

I suppose the primary matters with the rope drawings are the space, the figure in the space, and the how which are invited to sup at the same table. Speaking of space, I tracked down that quote, which I wrote in a letter to an Irish writer, Dorothy Walker:

> Space is a kind of jungle, a complete chaos with no rhyme or reason at all. The ropes draw temporary propositions that give brief visions of order. But the order is always lapsing into chaos again with new step. For the pieces change radically with even small moves. Thus they are to a degree unknowable—there's no single gestalt, just a succession of order and disorder. Eventually both of these conceptions proceed from the mind—the piece enables you to make your own order or disorder. There is no one right view.

This applies more to the work I did without painting the walls, and the emphasis on some sightlines and symmetries which came later in the seventies.

The more recent work—late seventies and eighties—takes the whole room and constructs sets of sightlines and projections that mobilize the walls and make the space perceptually—and thus psychologically—unstable, or stabilize it in ways that require some degree of losing constancies and learning yourself in a new space. Space, like water, is highly tractable, malleable, kind of stupid. It'll do anything you want if you know how to coax and not bully it. It will speak any words or sentences you want it to with the help of color, and it then speaks, spatializes, and colors you. It gets you out of the I–Thou situation and banishes that fashionable Other, or introduces you to different versions of yourself that are rarely alien. However, this is complicated, because sometimes seeing other people in the work varies between estrangement and community, and whenever I do a piece I call on that poor all-purpose spectator who has to haul itself out of bed and stagger into the gallery to get another workout. Recently, I've been taking the charged space that is house or domicile and playing a game of inside-outside-inside in terms of painted walls, doors, windows, and the basic cube or pyramid, which provokes retakes on the notion of location and where you were, are, will be, i.e., trying to incorporate the fractions of past and future into the now, which any half-way piece of good architecture does anyway.

We all have secret texts, I suppose, that accompany us in our voyages and I have to admit old Bishop Berkeley is one smart cookie for my money. His notebooks A and B are so full of astute comments about sight, blindness, perception, constructing the world, etc. that I fancy I see him in his clerical gown testing the rope pieces and questioning "if there be not two kinds of visible extension, one perceived by a confused view, the other by a distinct successive direction of the optic axis to each point." He and Locke are great to read (for my purposes) because their investigations into the senses do not isolate them, but are about the way the world and ourselves are composed by our (variable) perceptions. The stakes there are high, they are figuring out the very basis on which we presume to move and think and touch, etc. and are always exhilarating to read. I hate when this kind of thing is dismissed as "perceptual art" or some such moniker which sends the rest of our organism to some Siberian Gulag, while we entertain in the gallery with psychology textbook tricks.

Letter to Russell Panczenko
Director, Elvehjem Museum of Art, Madison, Wisconsin
June 29, 1992

Here are some categories onto which several of the objects in the exhibition fall:

GESTURES

Aspen 5/6: A collection of works (music, film, art, poetry, literature) and documents which dispose these works according to several layers of a conceptual framework, using historical documents/artworks (ancestors) and contemporary documents/artworks to create a field from which several readings can be made.

Past/Present/Future: A photograph of an abandoned shop front which reflects the stream of traffic (time) from three windows, two tilted at an angle from the sidewalk and one parallel to it. An extended commentary relentlessly notices the paradoxes in time created by this artifact—reversals, anticipations, predictions, scrambled memories, and gaps and leaps in the continuum.

Name Change: A documentation of the change from the artist Brian O'Doherty to the artist Patrick Ireland who undertakes to sign his works by this name "until such time as the British military presence is removed from Northern Ireland and all citizens are granted their civil rights."

Ireland: A Modest Proposal: In which the six occupied counties are relocated in the center of the remaining twenty-six, where they are assimilated, digested, and "become an indivisible part of the country."

Wittgenstein 8H–8B: A series of drawings in pencil (8H to 8B) showing the transformation of Wittgenstein's image (drawn from a photograph in *Encounter* magazine) as it rides from the extreme of the faintly linear to the extremely smudgy. Thereby asking a question of his likeness to which it provides sixteen answers. And thereby pointing out the degree to which changes in modes of representation (language) answer the question asked. Each of the sixteen images speaks his image differently while trying to give the same answer. Being in turn a comment on a profusion of contemporary references to Wittgenstein, most of which misunderstand him. Accepting for the moment the proposition that art is "language-like."

Between Categories: A work which tests and defines the limits of categories, borders, edges, zones, and the slippage between and across them. If categories are artificial, mental, and unknown in nature, they are a way of knowing, though what you ultimately know may be just categories—the taxonomic fallacy. The thing that a thing is most like is itself. When it begins to be unlike itself, it visits other categories, provoking hypotheses as it seeks its likeness in other objects as formulated by the senses. At a certain variable point it ceases to be itself and becomes something else, which it subsequently confirms. This process is illustrated as five sets of ten cards each change from one object to another. The series change within category (teapot to bowl), between categories (house to mouse), from thing to language (key to THE) and from something to nothing (blob). The mind's most urgent need—to recognize—equivocates between order (category) and disorder (loss of category), as memory tests itself against present experience. Proposition: a category of totally unlike things.

Duchamp Portrait: A multipart work in which Marcel Duchamp's heartbeat is stolen and secured in an electrocardiogram and animated in three oscilloscopes, two at resting heartrate and one with heartrate slowed down to 17 per minute. With attendant records and drawings.

CHESS SERIES

The alert, purposeful wanderings of the chess pieces, each with its own demeanor, are limited by the usual arbitrary rules (all rules in games are arbitrary, I guess). Each chessman (and woman/queen) has its own area of surveillance and can't go outside it. Strategy opens sudden pathways and corridors on the board's highly conceptualized killing field.

I made the chess set with each piece's choreographic program in mind. The rooks shunt front and sideways on right-angled pathways. To the bishop, cutting obliquely across the grid, half the board is unavailable. The knights stammer along in their crooked way, often engineering a surprise as they leap over friend and enemy, the only pieces with this airborne capacity. Neutered pawns shuffle forward after their first double step and kill out of the corner of their eyes. Each has the potential to suffer an enormous gender change. The king, target and ceremonial victim of all the intrigue, is impotent beyond a single disabled step. And the queen, mighty in her powers, defender of her gelded consort, ruthlessly seeks out his other. Arrogant in her powers, she projects laserlike threats to any quarter of the board. Only the knight's crooked high jump is beyond her. Flanked by church and state (king and bishop), she doesn't understand him anyway. He can kill her across covering defenders. In fact anyone can kill anyone and does as casualties mount to the end game. But not to the death. For the checkmated king never dies. The murderous scheming ends in surrender. Occasionally the bloody war of attrition ends in a paralysed equilibrium. The board freezes. Neither wins.

I guess I was more interested in the idea of chess and the great chess masters than in the game itself, which I wasn't very good at. I studied Paul Morphy and spoke with Duchamp quite a bit. Harold Schoenberg, the former music critic of the *New York Times*, who used to play with Duchamp, said he was a fine player but not great. At Duchamp's request I did a *Knight's Box* for the chess foundation (in 1967).

The tangle of moves accumulating invisibly on the board as a game matured fascinated me, and I drew some from famous games until they yielded a superimposed labyrinth of tracks—a graph of consciousness that looked chaotic. I color-coded the pieces and the tangle got more interesting. Ways of graphing movement led me to other modes of notation. From the chessboard came the structural plays.

OGHAM DRAWINGS AND SCULPTURES

In 1967, I began a series of drawings and sculptures incorporating language, mirroring, symmetry/asymmetry, placement, and repetition. The language was an ancient sign system called *ogham*, a fifth-century adaption of twenty letters of the Roman alphabet. Denoted by strokes across a corner or line, the ogham alphabet has similarities to serial music (see below).

By scoring the language across edges and corners, I evolved a repertory of word, image, and object on a reflective ground that frequently doubled and reversed the possible readings. The complexities of these works are belied by their minimal appearances. Among their themes are the relationship between word and object, the idea of word as action, of repetition modified by placement, interval, and reflection, and, since the sculptures could be "read," the relationship of sound to structure—as relevant (or irrelevant) as that of sound to meaning.

A major theme was the viewer's relationship to his or her mirrored image. Some works exclude the viewer ("to look into the mirror and see no reflection"), or double his or her image, or so reverse it that the reflected space within the sculpture became continuous with that of the space in which the viewer stands. Thus, in the "W" sculptures, the viewer sees his or her image in a "real" space, may shake hands with themselves or, in walking past the sculpture, may watch his or her image change direction and meet itself as it flows across a word or words.

Few words (and occasionally numbers) were used in the sculptures. The prime usages were vowels, and the words *One*, *Here*, *Now*. The Vowel Works (including *Golden Vowels*) relate directly to the vowel poems I wrote and read in the late sixties.

One/One/One (1969) in this exhibition joins two inscribed ones, read from top down and bottom up, in one sculpture; reflections add two other *Ones*. *Golden Vowels* (1968) reads OOUEIAEE. *Here* (1969/70) deploys a system of three columns of "here's" plus a fourth reflected column in a space where each "here," when focused on, throws the others into a different configuration. *Meribah* (1970), the place where Moses rod struck the rock which then gushed water, runs that action up and down the vertical column by giving two directions to the word itself, and its reflection.

Letter to Russell Panczenko, Director
Elvehjem Museum of Art, Madison, Wisconsin
August 27, 1992

Here's a list of the rope drawings to date. I'm also enclosing some material on labyrinths. I'm busily retrieving what I can from the shards and rubble of the past. It's amazing how much has disappeared. And when it surfaces in the chaos of the studio, how much it needs to be spruced up, its dusty face polished . . . I'm getting to work on the colors for the installation . . . I'm also at work on a large isometric drawing of our grand labyrinth . . .

ROPE DRAWINGS 1973–1992

1. *Phonic Grid*, 112 Greene Street, New York, May 1973
2. *Cradle*, Betty Parsons Gallery, New York, January 1974
3. *Newton's Rings*, The Clocktower, New York, May 1974
4. Untitled, Studio, New York, November 1974
5. *One Drawing in Two Rooms*, Los Angeles County Museum of Art, January 1975
6. *One Triangle, Three Ones*, Los Angeles County Museum of Art, January 1975
7. Untitled, 112 Greene Street, New York, April 1975
8. Untitled, 112 Greene Street, New York, April 1975
9. *Inverted Pyramid*, 112 Greene Street, New York, April 1975
10. Untitled, private collection, Philadelphia, April 1975
11. *Skywalker*, Hopkins Center, Dartmouth College, New Hampshire, April 1975
12. Untitled, David Hendricks Gallery, Dublin, Ireland, August 1975
13. *Sky Light*, Wright State University, Dayton, Ohio, November 1975
14. *Sky Mark*, Wright State University, Dayton, Ohio, November 1975
15. *Corner*, School of Visual Arts Museum, New York, December 1975
16. Untitled, Philadelphia College of Art, Philadelphia, February 1976
17. Untitled, Studio, New York, April 1976
18. Untitled, Hirshhorn Museum, Washington, D. C. , May 1976
19. *Standing Magic Square*, P.S. 1, Institute for Art and Urban Resources, New York, June 1976
20. *Papillon*, Courthouse Square, Dayton, Ohio, June 1976
21. *Yellow Light*, private collection, Todi, Italy, July 1976
22. *The L in the Triangle*, private collection, Todi, Italy, July 1976
23. Untitled, Heath Gallery, Atlanta, September 1976
24. Untitled, Heath Gallery, Atlanta, Georgia, September 1976
25. *Stairwell*, Max Protetch Gallery, Washington, D.C., December 1976
26. *Screen I*, Max Protetch Gallery, Washington, D.C., December 1976
27. *Screen II*, Max Protetch Gallery, Washington, D.C., December 1976
28. Untitled, Max Protetch Gallery, Washington, D.C., December 1976
29. Untitled, Moore College of Art, Philadelphia, January 1977
30. *Inverted Pyramid*, La Jolla Museum of Contemporary Art, San Diego, January 1977
31. *Corner Line*, La Jolla Museum of Contemporary Art, San Diego, January 1977
32. *Floating VW*, La Jolla Museum of Contemporary Art, San Diego, January 1977

33. Untitled, La Jolla Museum of Contemporary Art, San Diego, January 1977

34. *Yellow Rectangle, Rosc*, Hugh Lane Gallery of Modern Art, Dublin, Ireland, September 1977

35. *Thin Drawing*, Seattle Art Museum, Seattle, October 1977

36. *Two Blind Spots*, Seattle Art Museum, Seattle, October 1977

37. Untitled, Seattle Art Museum, Seattle, October 1977

38. Untitled, Seattle Art Museum, Seattle, October 1977

39. Untitled, Studio, New York, November 1977

40. *Camera*, School of Visual Arts Museum, New York, April 1978

41. *Wallenda*, Gallery, University of Ohio, Columbus, May 1978

42. *On the Edge*, Contemporary Art Center, Cincinnati, Ohio, May 1978

43. Untitled, Contemporary Art Center, Cincinnati, Ohio, May 1978

44. *Casino*, Deauville, France, September 1978

45. *Raum*, Galerie December, Dusseldorf, Germany, September 1978

46. *Yellow Square*, Max Protetch Gallery, New York, February 1979

47. Untitled, P.S. 1, New York, February 1979

48. *Cornered*, Project Gallery, Dublin, Ireland, March 1979

49. *Floating Pyramid*, Hansen-Fuller Gallery, San Francisco, June 1979

50. *Inside-out Room*, University Art Museum, Berkeley, California, June 1979

51. *Cinemascope*, University Art Museum, Berkeley, California, July 1979

52. *Corner for Tatlin and Fred Astaire*, Hayden Gallery, M. I. T., September 1979

53. *Untitled Corner*, Hayden Gallery, M. I. T., September 1979

54. Untitled, Hudson River Museum, New York October 1979

55. Untitled, Landmark Center, St. Paul, Minnesota, January 1980

56. *Red Room*, Spencer Museum, University of Kansas, Lawrence, March 1980

57. *Borromini's Underpass*, Akron Art Museum, Akron, Ohio, April 1980

58. *Borromini's Portal*, Charles Cowles Gallery, New York, September, 1980

59. Untitled, Washington Project for the Arts, Washington, D.C., October 1980

60. Untitled, Studio, New York, December 1980

61. *Without Ropes*, Cranbrook Academy, Detroit, February 1981

62. *Catenary*, Fogg Art Museum, Cambridge, Mass., May 1981

63. Untitled, Lodz, Poland, October, 1981

64. *String Quartet (4 Corners)*, The Brooklyn Museum, New York, May 1982

65. *Roof Garden*, private collection, New York, October 1982

66. *Double Up in Blue and Grey*, Studio, Washington, D.C., December 1982

67. *Rimbaud's Cradle*, Charles Cowles Gallery, New York, February 1983

68. *Eddie's Window*, The Grey Art Gallery, New York University, June 1983

69. *Blue Room*, The Butler Institute of American Art, Youngstown, Ohio, October 1983

70. *Kane*, Charles Cowles Gallery, New York, February 1984

71. *Big A*, University of Virginia, Charlottesville, April 1984

72. *Double Scoop*, Studio, New York, November 1984

73. *Purgatory of Humphrey Chimpden Earwicker, Homunculus, Four Spatial /Verbal Propositions*, Hyde Gallery, Trinity College, Dublin, Ireland, February 1985

74. *Dark Corner*, private collection, Todi, Italy, July 1985

75. Untitled, private collection, Washington, D.C., November 1985

76. *Present Conditional*, National Museum of American Art, Washington, D.C., April 1986

77. *House Call, Martello Terrace*, Clocktower, New York, September 1986

78. *Two-D in Three-D*, Clocktower, New York, September 1986

79. *In Memoriam*, Kent State University, Kent, Ohio, September 1986

80. *The Tennis Court Oath*, Kent State University, Kent, Ohio, September 1986

81. *Remote Control*, Galerie Hoffman, Friedberg, Germany, October 1986

82. *End Zone*, Charles Cowles Gallery, New York, December 1986

83. *Petra*, The Detroit Institute of Arts, May 1987

84. *Women of Algiers*, The Detroit Institute of Arts, May 1987

85. *Trecento*, private collection, Todi, Italy, July 1987

86. *Morton's Journey*, Artspace, San Francisco, September 1987

87. Untitled, private collection, Washington, D.C., October 1987

88. *Rear-View Mirror*, Studio, New York, December 1987

89. *Peacekeeper*, Montgomery Museum of Art, Ala., September 1988

90. *Red H*, Studio, New York, April 1989

91. *DIAID: In Memory of Lost Friends*, Fuller Gross Gallery, San Francisco, May 1989

92. *H-Block*, Orpheus Gallery, Belfast, Northern Ireland, June 1989

93. *East/West*, Galerie Hoffman, Friedberg, Germany, March 1990

94. *Inverted Pyramid for Cyclops*, Charles Cowles Gallery, New York, September 1990

95. *White Column*, Studio, New York, November 1990

96. *Fountain II*, private collection, Todi, Italy, July 1991

97. *Ingeborg's Egyptian "I,"* The Detroit Institute of Arts, June 1992

98. *Omphalos*, Elvehjem Museum of Art, Madison, Wis., November 1992

99. *Caligari's Palace*, Institute of Contemporary Art, P.S. 1, New York, April 1993

Letter to Russell Panczenko
Director, Elvehjem Museum of Art, Madison, Wisconsin
November, 1992

You asked me about the open box drawings and whence they came. I spent a lot of time opening and closing "boxes" in the 1980s, particularly in the early part of the decade. I don't know when they started—in the late 1970s, I suppose.

Cubes are kind of dumb. They sit there and look at you, which is their great virtue. Any question you ask a cube, it gives you the same answer ("I'm solid and I've got six sides, and if you don't believe me, make me transparent. I'll show you the other three."). They are great for illusions of solidity, permanence, weight, and cast a good shadow. In the 1970s I drew lines, Xs, angles, zig-zags, etc.—the usual repertory of marks—on the six planes. The outline of the "box" or cube was drawn lightly so that the lines would first appear flat on the surface, then obligingly dispose themselves in space when you copped on to the faint outline of the cube. Then you could spend your time shuttling between two and three dimensions, between which a lot of good art stands. The *Inside the Cube* book in the exhibition is based on this idea, though there the cube outline is clear as day. Barbara isn't mad about many of these drawings, but I like them a lot. They gave me a push from the flat "I" drawings etc. towards the third dimension, or more accurately, towards what represents it. So they allowed me to isolate for my purposes the essence of that "three dimensions represented on two" tradition, which goes back (in perspective lines of time?) a long way, as we know. Maybe they gave me an opportunity to say something mildly new about the cube through epigram and ellipsis. At least I hope so (there's nothing worse than a failed epigram).

Out of this came (as artists say in semi-biblical fashion about their own work) the open boxes, which simply swing out the cube's (or box's) six planes. And what great fun that was! Sometimes when you open a door you can romp around for a while, until your shadow sneaks in, catches up with you, and makes things difficult again. You can see that in your exhibition. First the pencil drawings of twelve planes (six of the cube and six of the opened sides); then a lot of dense watercolors of the open boxes in sullen colors; then finally the labor-intensive drawings in which the poor hand is imprisoned in an idea and doesn't get out until it has served its time. (don't do too many of these—or the installation drawings—anymore because my eyes give out before my hand). In these drawings, you could sophisticate the color by threading the planes with different strands, play opacity against transparency, and all the time stay in touch with the onlooker (or looker at-er) because of the subject: the box, which is as much—and as little—a subject as a jug. Everyone has opened a box at some time, and boxes have secrets. But true to my demythologizing (minimal) origins, these boxes don't have any sense of enclosure or exclusion. But they do speak of two/three dimensions in a voice as clear (I hope) as crystal. The execution of the work modifies that with a chorus of colors, ambiguous readings (which open plane snaps back into which side?), and logical but arbitrary perspectives introduced by the isometric (antiperspectival) nature of the skeletal cube.

There is also—if you have an active, curious (God bless them) viewer—a sort of mumble of low-grade process (figuring out what goes where), interrupted by the imagined sound of open sides slapping neatly into their mother cube. But this is just gravy. First and last, they're drawings. Since the devil sometimes urges you on, I superimposed two open boxes (there's one in the show) to torture and exhilarate the perfect viewer, who will follow you anywhere. Sometimes you quickly exhaust a new idea. But I still return to the open boxes now and then with pleasure and delight. For years I tried to do a rope drawing of an open box and painted walls that would work. I think I've got it and will test it in the studio shortly.

Barbara read this letter and reminded me that boxes of one kind or another have always ducked in and out of my work, and in truth they have; even the rope drawings stretch themselves out in the gallery box. I'm sure there's no shortage of Freudiana that could be unloaded into the box concern, then wrapped up and immobilized as followers of the Viennese pedant tend to do. But these flying boxes of the eighties open their wings with nothing whatever to hide, and free of gravity, solicit different moods as their variable angles joyfully invent the space in which they fly.

Letter to Jan van der Marck
Chief Curator and Curator of Twentieth-century Art, The Detroit Institute of Arts
November, 1992

I'm delighted you're writing the Elvehjem catalogue. Your support for my work goes back a long way—not to speak of your loyalty when work you admire is under attack. Of that I have first-hand knowledge. I hope the work doesn't shuffle its feet and look embarrassed under your uncompromising scrutiny. Speaking of writing: I keep waiting for your collection. I first read your writing in a Walker catalogue years ago. What you wrote was so far from the pious ejaculations of cataloguese that I sat up immediately. I don't remember words and phrases now, but almost thirty years later I still have a sense of the gliding ease, the sudden ignition of phrases and imaginative reach that spun the work through the museum walls into the wilderness of objects and occurrences outside.

Going around the Wisconsin show—playing Virgil to your Dante—was a rare pleasure. Many of what I call the "gestures" haven't been seen before—a gesture being a one-time, time-bound quasi-didactic message/opportunity implicating art. Some went public (*Aspen, Duchamp Portrait, Wittgenstein*) since gestures presume an audience. *The Critic's Shoes* were kept in the dark, since I wasn't keen to remind people of a critical past that might cripple my new-born (in the U.S.) young artist. I tried several versions of the shoes until I got what seemed to me the right one. I had a fantasy of walking in shoes sheathed and abuzz with words through the uptown grid of galleries (there wasn't any Soho then), bearing language (criticism) to the wordless (art)— giving it the doubtful gift of tongues. My verbal (and as it happens, tongueless) shoes had walked me all over Manhattan and these sometimes dolorous rounds had led me to salutary meditations on man as an object-producing creature. So making these asymmetrically symmetrical twin objects speak seemed slightly cynical and funny at the time. Now they look like corpses, interred in dead words.

But the words, if you read them randomly (since the criticism is cut and collaged) mumble and grouse and stutter aphasiacally as their paper-thin cortical layer follows the contours of their support—the shoes that in turn supported me and paid my rent. I wish sometimes I could walk those shoes back to 1964 and be much smarter than I was then.

Reading the shoes at the opening had some of the dolor of opening old magazines—names forgotten or now celebrated, my own naivetés and occasional insights, dead galleries and bright hopes, young lions and old heroes, movements being born, stilled, and frozen into their allotted quota of time. And finally there was the folly of making the shoes bear witness to their own journeys, as they run after art, catch up with it, and become what they pursued.

I've had a lot of category trouble in my life (doctor, tinker, tailor). Speaking of categories, I remember, in 1957, staring at the whitewashed walls of the Nissen hut which was part of the experimental psychology labs in Cambridge [England], wondering how to design an experiment and earn my keep. Exp. Psy. was a fascinating field until it got eaten up by mathematics. I liked it when it had a down-home aspect—take a piece of conventional wisdom (e.g., old people are rigid) and prove it true or false.

I'd wanted to work with a man named Thouless who had done remarkable work on "constancies"—the way an idea structures a set of perceptions so that the world doesn't collapse into a restless flux that unnames everything. The idea "cup," for instance, stabilizes a wide variety of cup shapes that fall within that category. So I began to think of categories. When does one thing become another? Or not itself? What is like and unlike? How many categories can one thing visit? I made several series of ten carcs each in which one object turns into another through intermediate stages—stool into fire-irons car to mouse, key into the word THE.

I tested these cards against two groups—young and aged. Was the rumored rigidity of the old to new ideas true or false? The stations at which changes took place became clear: the point where an identification was abandoned; the zone where what is seen is unknown; the zone where new hypotheses are offered; and the point at which the new recognition takes place. The experiment offered as much information about how old and young view such tests as it did about its primary aim, which, by the way, was more favorable to the aged group than expected.

In 1968—eleven years later—I came across the cards in a drawer and there was no hesitation. In the *Aspen* I'd done the previous year I'd posited a category of *Between Categories*, which so delighted Morty Feldman that he immeciately gave that name to a new composition (in those days, Morty and I were inseparable).

So it seemed natural to subsume the cards as "art," accompanied by my notes of the time, a report on my experiment in a book called *Ageing and Human Skill* by my mentor, Alan T. Welford of St. John's College (a darlin' man), and my 1968 meditations on the nature of categories, which now more than ever seemed to me a master key to how we structure the world so that we can "understand" it. All categories being, of course, as artificial as a straight line in nature. So categories began to reflect back not just the apples and oranges of our casual categorizations, but assumptions, false logic, defective syntheses, prejudices, rationales, delusions, laws. What happens at the edges of categories? Where do you draw the line? When are like things unlike? My absurdly low-tech experiment had colonized (as transparently simple things sometimes do) a larger archipelago of idea than expected, so I spent some time chasing ideas around and into the slots, crevasses, and pigeon-holes of my mind to bring home what would now (I suppose) be called an early conceptual piece.

I'd visited the category business the year before in the *Aspen* box, where I posited flexible sets of categories, "movements," etc. to trap the contents of the box in different configurations. The conceptual scheme was laid out in the folded contents page. I needed a text to give it some closure. After failing to find what I wanted, I made up a quote from a fictitious book, *Language as Placement* by Sigmund Bode, an alias I'd used before. The text referred to the juxtapositions and contiguities of the boxed contributors—a *festschrift* of authors I'd commissioned and commandeered (with a young man's cheek and confidence) to dance to my music. I added several members of the group I was seeing a lot of—a presumptuousness time has dealt with more or less kindly. The sense of an open end, of inheriting ancestors, of honoring and questioning those who, however indirectly, were confirming our particular journey, was very much on my mind. As were Morty Feldman's many admonitions about "passing through" New York, i.e., becoming a New York artist in a strenuous rite of passage through its postwar past. That box was for me the equivalent of ceremonial scarification. It enabled me to take a firm step forward into an arena I had entered (with my first one-man show at Byron) a year before, taking a bit of trashing from several sides (which also made me feel properly blooded).

The Wittgenstein portrait was a category too, a category of Wittgensteins. How did it come about? There is often a time in avant-gardes when a book takes on a talismanic presence. Kubler's *Shape of Time* was one of those for a while (indeed it stimulated me to ask him for a contribution to the *Aspen*). You remember though, that Wittgenstein's Brown and Black Books were much quoted in the late sixties, and his name became a reified object to toss around. Early conceptualism (I believe) benefited from his linguistic discriminations. Jasper Johns, with his usual intelligence, made hay with some of that. I got fed up with hearing Wittgenstein on every tongue, not always with much understanding. So I decided to "say" Wittgenstein in fourteen ways, drawing his image (taken from a photograph in *Encounter* magazine) with pencils from 7H to 7B. If, according to Wittgenstein, our questions presume, preempt, and generally determine the answers (so that questions need to be rephrased into answerable and not unanswerable propositions), I was asking Wittgenstein's image to answer my fourteen questions. They were all Wittgenstein, but no two Wittgenstein's were alike. The image changed ever so slightly (a function of my attempt at fidelity to the photograph). But the way it was depicted (said) also changed, since the nature of the question (the pencil) dictated to some degree the answer (the drawing). 7H was a faint, linear Wittgenstein. 7B was a messy, contrasty Wittgenstein. Was one Wittgenstein more Wittgenstein than another? How much variation was possible before he became not-Wittgenstein? Perhaps this seems a little too playful and period now, but I hope it preserves some wit.

I seem to be talking a lot about categories, but if you start concentrating on them, they seem to determine our views of each other, our prejudices, our art. The uncategorizable is uncomfortable. You know the slightly glazed/suspicious stare of someone who can't "place" you? Looking back (at least today) categories seem to shoot their vectors, limits, and borders through much of those early gestures. I don't know if you noticed the small *Kip's Bay: The Body and Its Discontents*? I found this small rectangular box with six registers of ten spaces filled with little wooden blocks. What function it served originally I have no idea. I played with it by making it a kind of surrogate body. On one of the four faces of the sixty wooden blocks (colored red), I inscribed an anatomical litany. From there I went counterclockwise to the next face (yellow), where I listed organs of sense. On the next (white), I placed the body's products and functions—physiology (how the anatomy works). On the last (blue), went the sinister registers of our decay and disasters—pathology. When you spilled them out of their slots, then randomly reinserted them, various scenarios of the body appeared like chimeras. A quick scan of these scenarios (for me, at least) brought home vistas of hospital beds, massive textbooks, dissecting rooms, ghosts of professors, deaths and resurrections. Also, a lexicon of names, various homunculi who get their monikers attached to some minute fragment of the body or its ills. This was done while I was at *The New York Times*. There's another half to this work, but about twenty of the blocks are missing and I couldn't restore it in time).

There is much more to be said, but time is on our heels and I look forward to our Monday meeting. There were, unfortunately, things I couldn't find for the exhibition—the film *Black* (I have the drawing but not the page by page transparent "book" that goes with it; the pseudo-manifesto of the mid-seventies, signed by my six alter egos; the wooden *Art Since 1945* book now at the Hirshhorn; the talking book started in 1966 and never finished because there were no audio cassettes then; the Dublin/New York language piece; the photographic self-portrait begun in 1969, etc.) Things swim up from the chaos of the studio, then they lapse back into the chaos again. Russell was relentless in that he made me root around, and kept saying "What is that?" I would answer "It's nothing," and he would insist on seeing it. As Barbara says, I need an artist's wife, but then she needs a wife too. And speaking of wives, my best to Sheila. Tell her I'm sorry about the Lions, even with Barry Sanders they're a sad—and worse—unlucky lot.

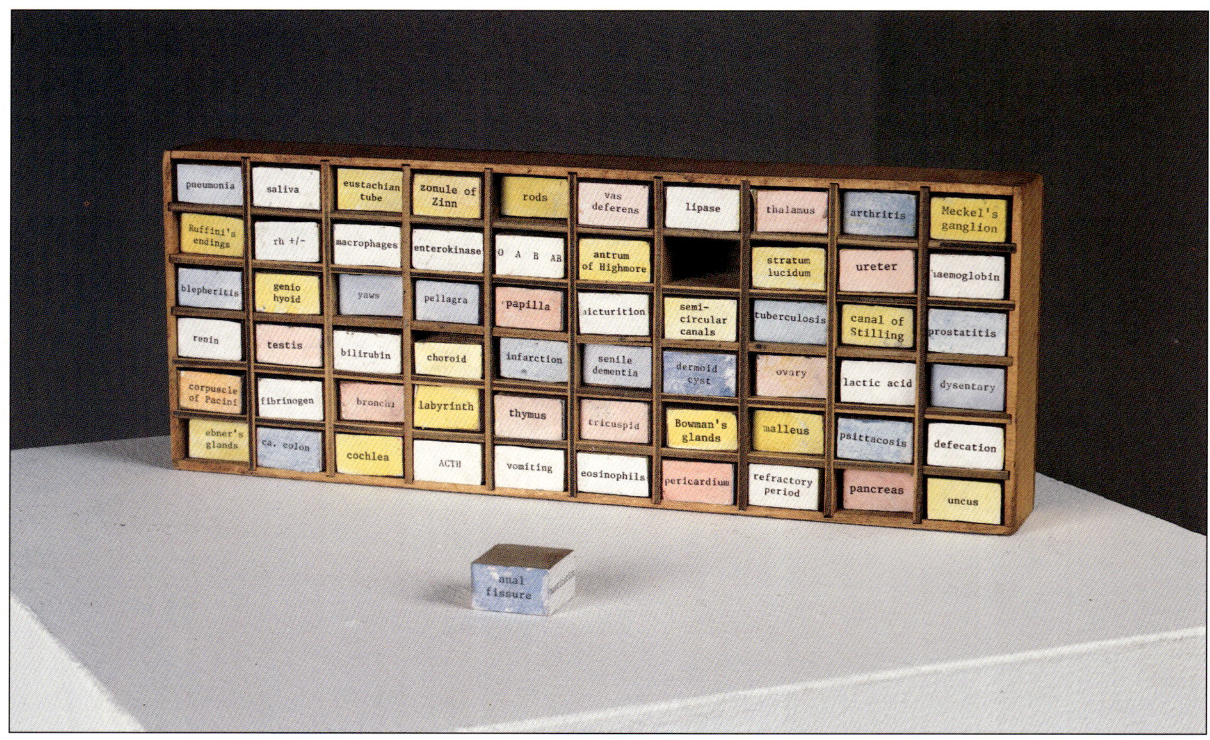

Word Works: *Kips Bay: The Body and Its Discontents*, 1964
Mixed media, 4 1/8 x 11 x 1 1/2 in.
Collection of the artist

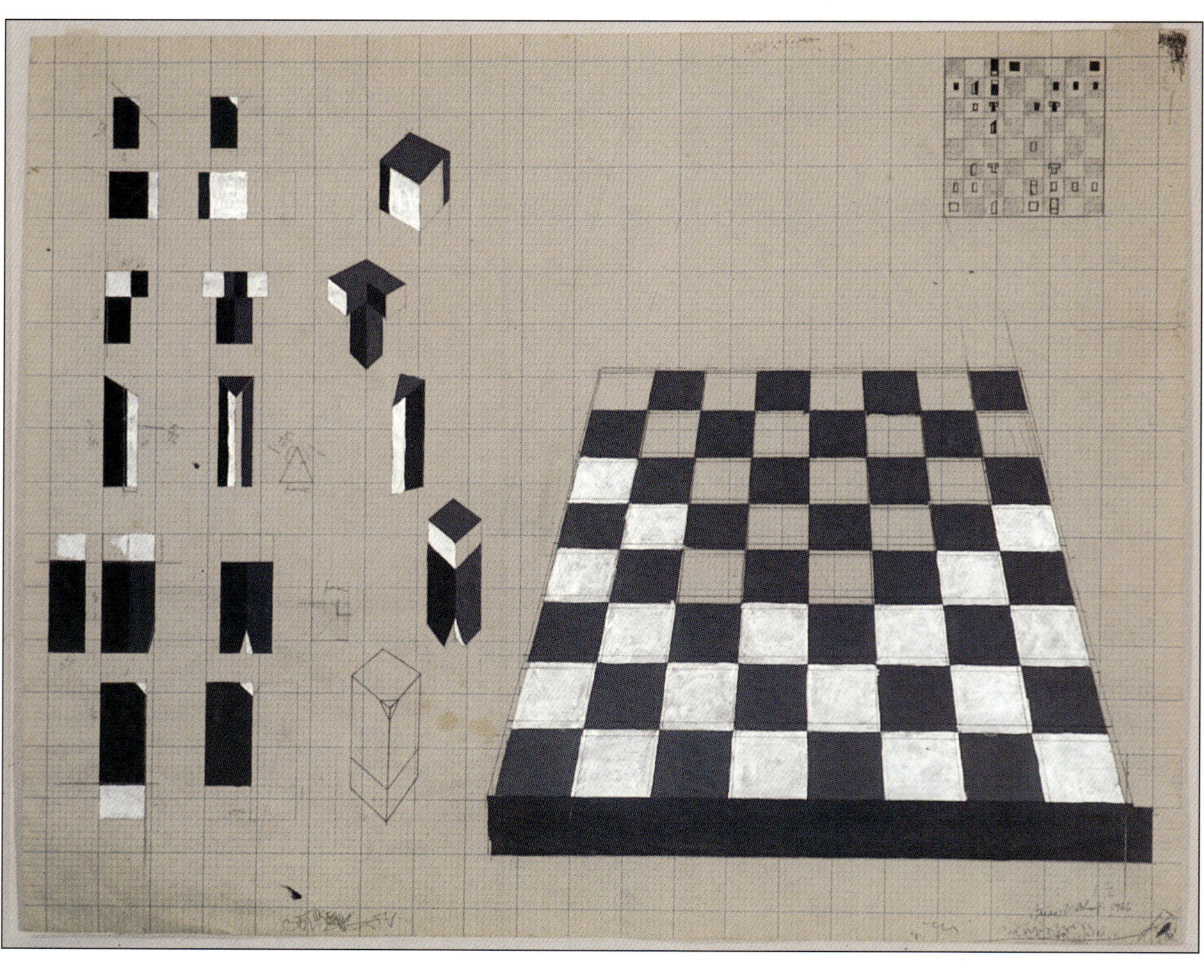

Chess Series: Chess set, 1966
Pen, gouache on graph paper, 17 x 22 in.
Collection of the artist

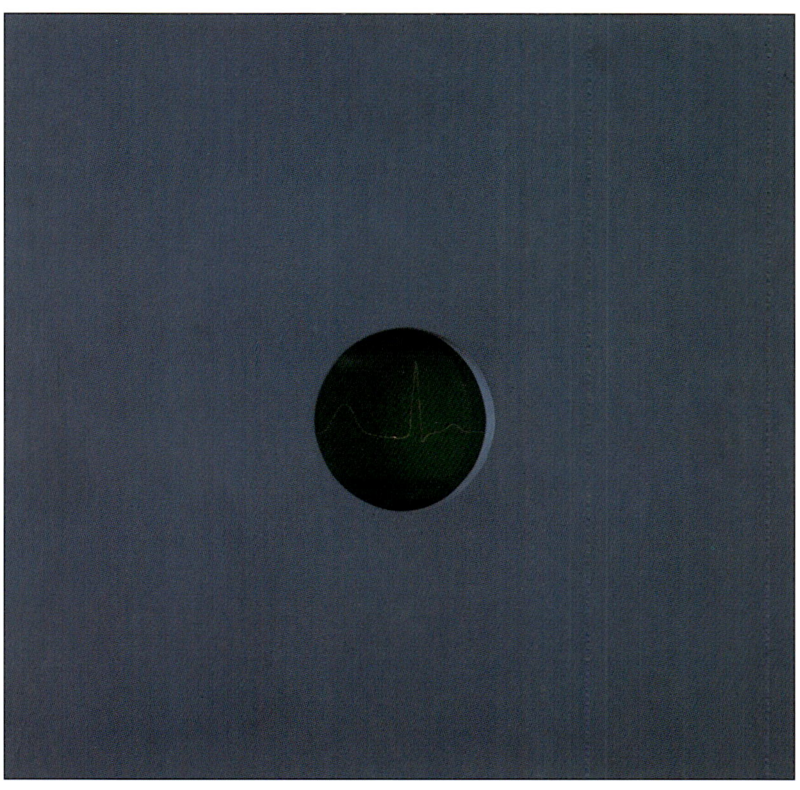

Gestures: Portrait of Marcel Duchamp: Slow Pulse Rate, 1966
Mixed media, 16 5/8 x 16 5/8 x 8 in.
Collecion of the artist

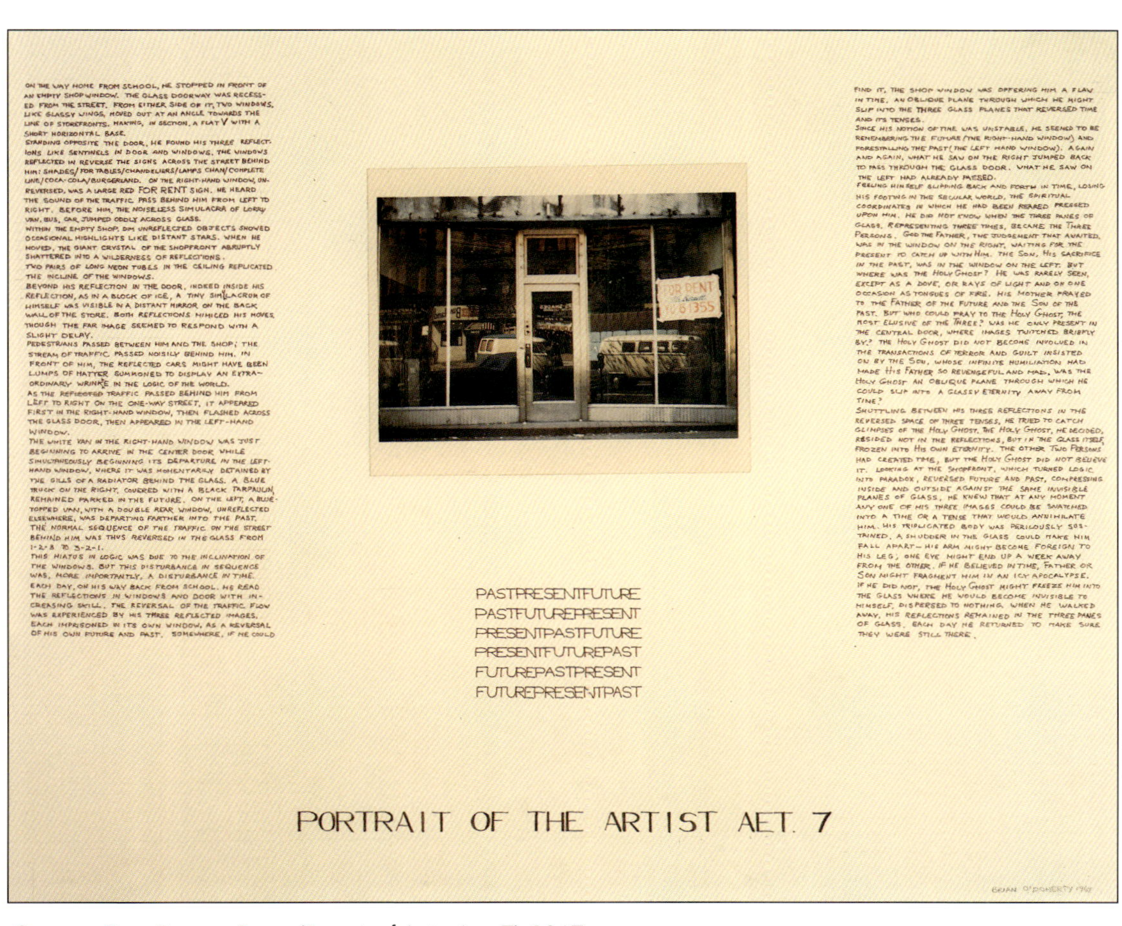

Gestures: Past, Present, Future (Portrait of Artist Aet. 7), 1967
Photo and text on posterboard, 23 x 29 in.
Collection of the artist

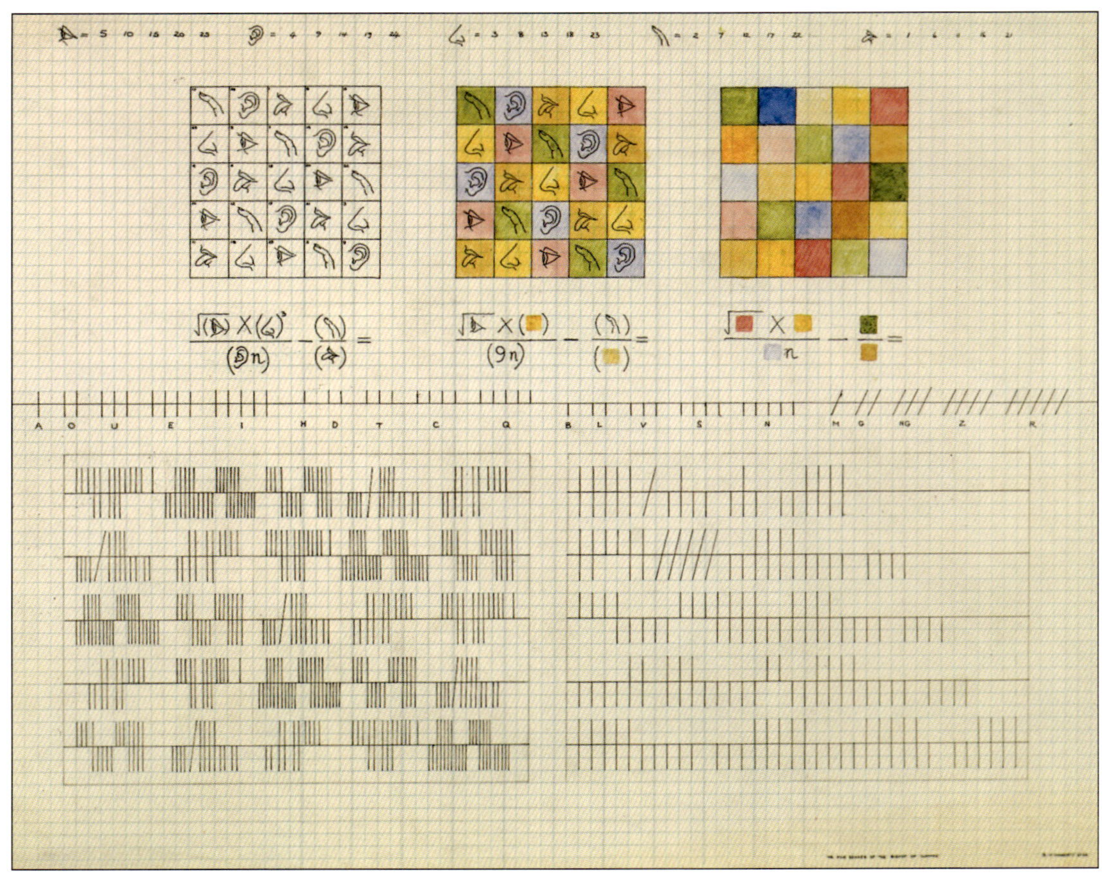

The Five Senses of the Bishop of Cloyne, 1967–68
Ink and watercolor on graph paper, 17 x 22 in.
Collection of the artist

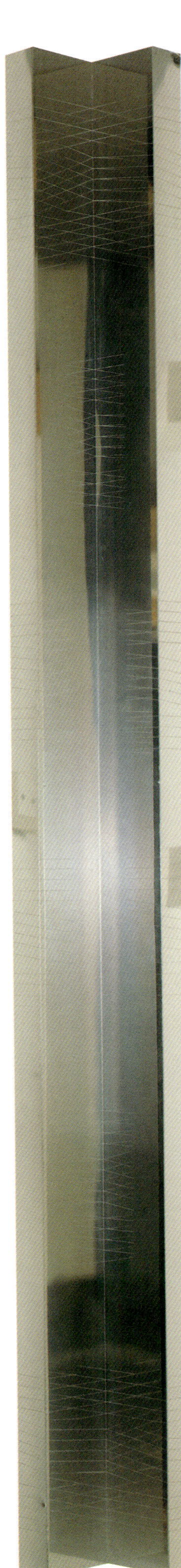

Ogham Sculptures: Annso (Here), 1970
Polished aluminum on wood, 72 x 8 1/2 x 4 1/4 in.
Elvehjem Musuem of Art Endowment Fund,
Juli Plant Grainger Endowment Fund,
Cyril W. Nave Endowment Fund purchase, 1992.335

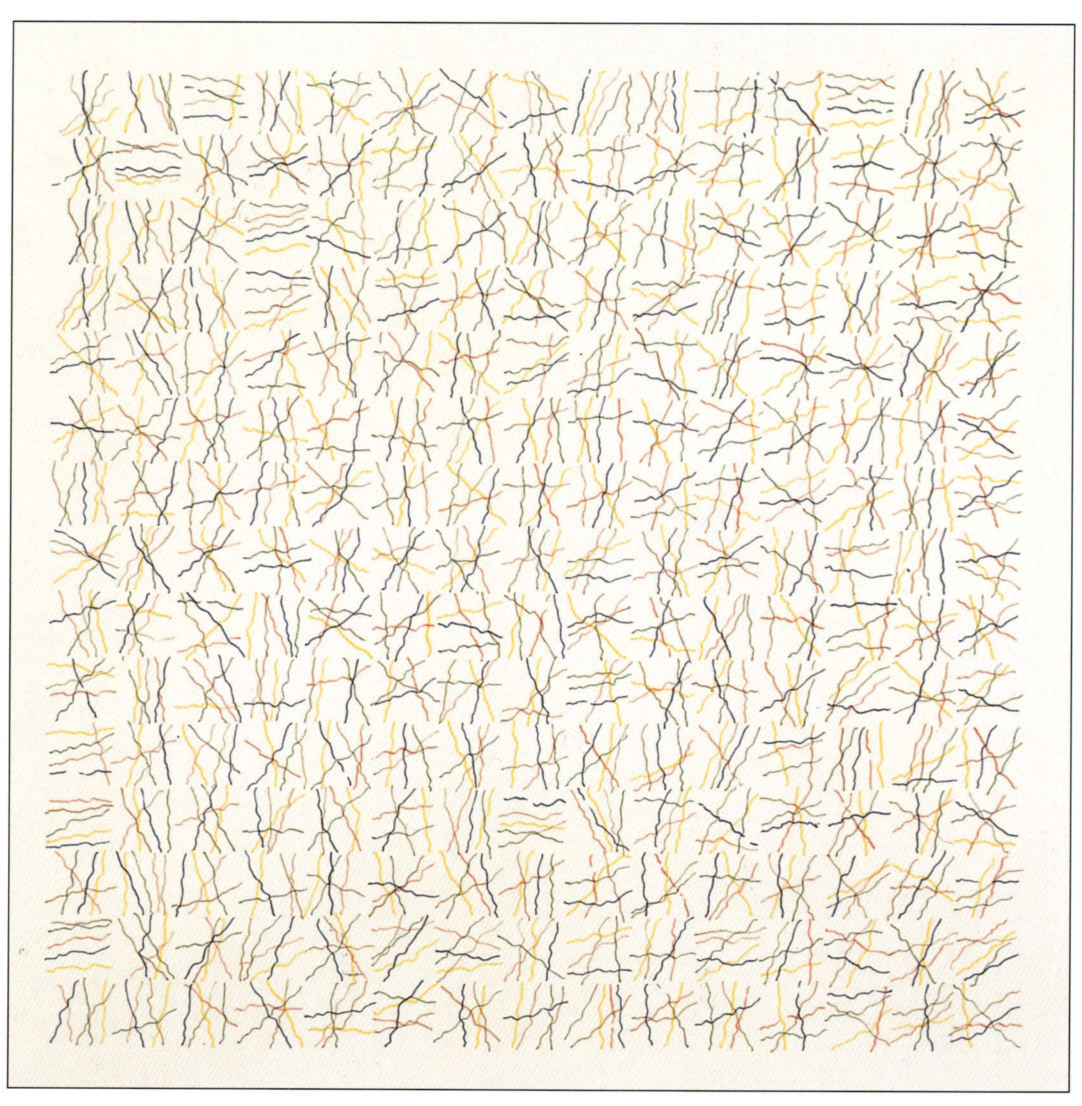

"I" Drawings: 225 I's, Overlapping Crooked Lines, 1971
Colored inks on paper, 23 x 29 in.
Collection of the artist

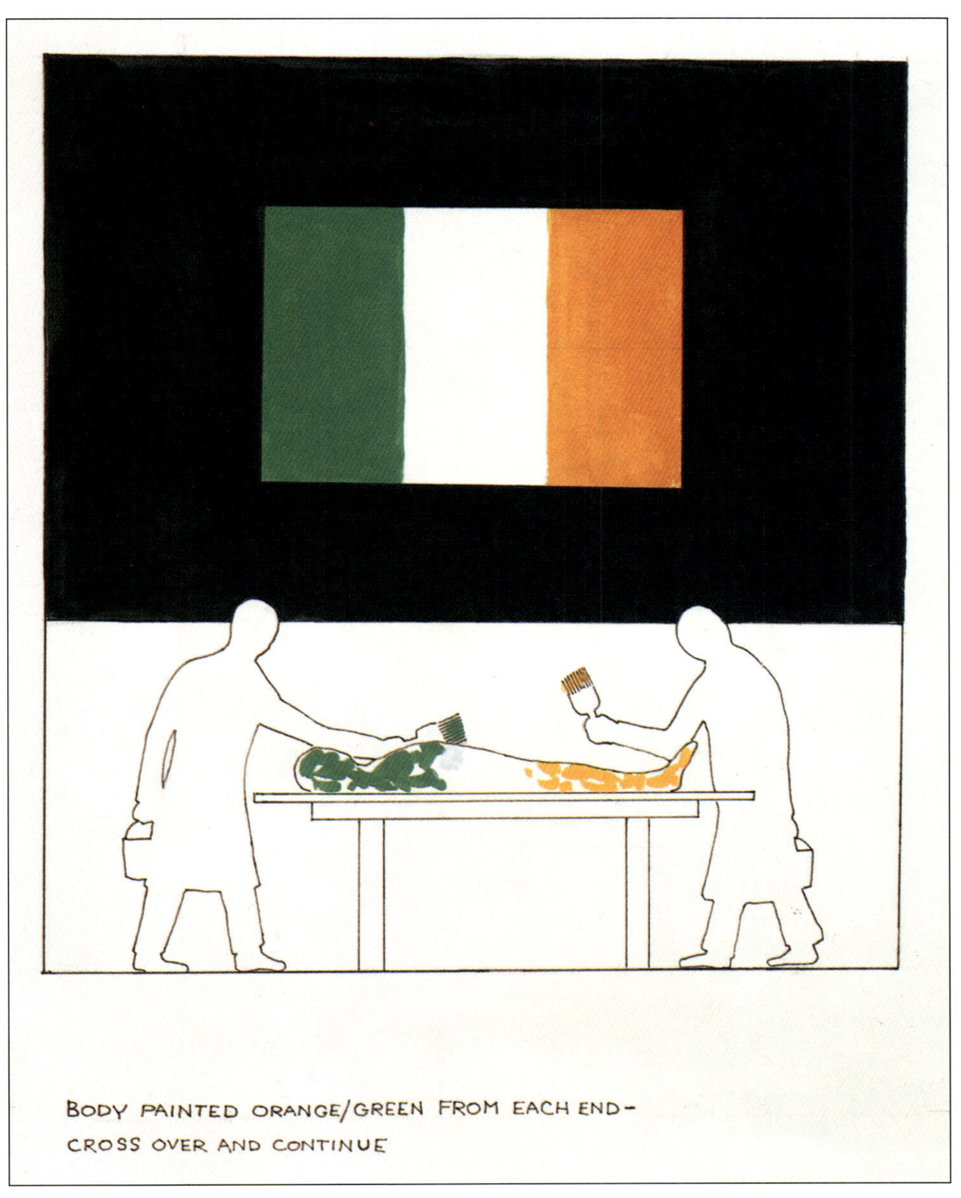

Gestures: Name Change (Detail), 1972
Photographs, ink and gouache drawings on paper, typed text on paper collaged onto posterboard, 27 7/8 x 60 in.
Collection of the artist

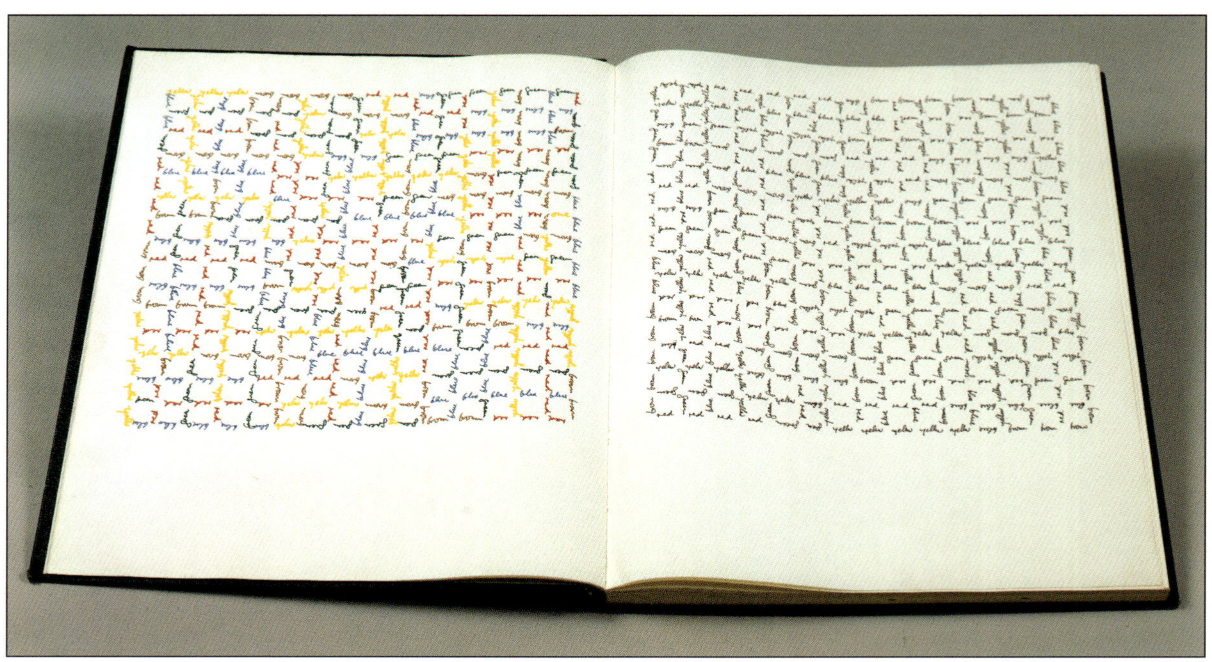

Artist's Books: The Book of Rope Drawing: Vowel Grid with Words, 1973
Colored inks on paper, 13 x 9 in.
Collection of the artist

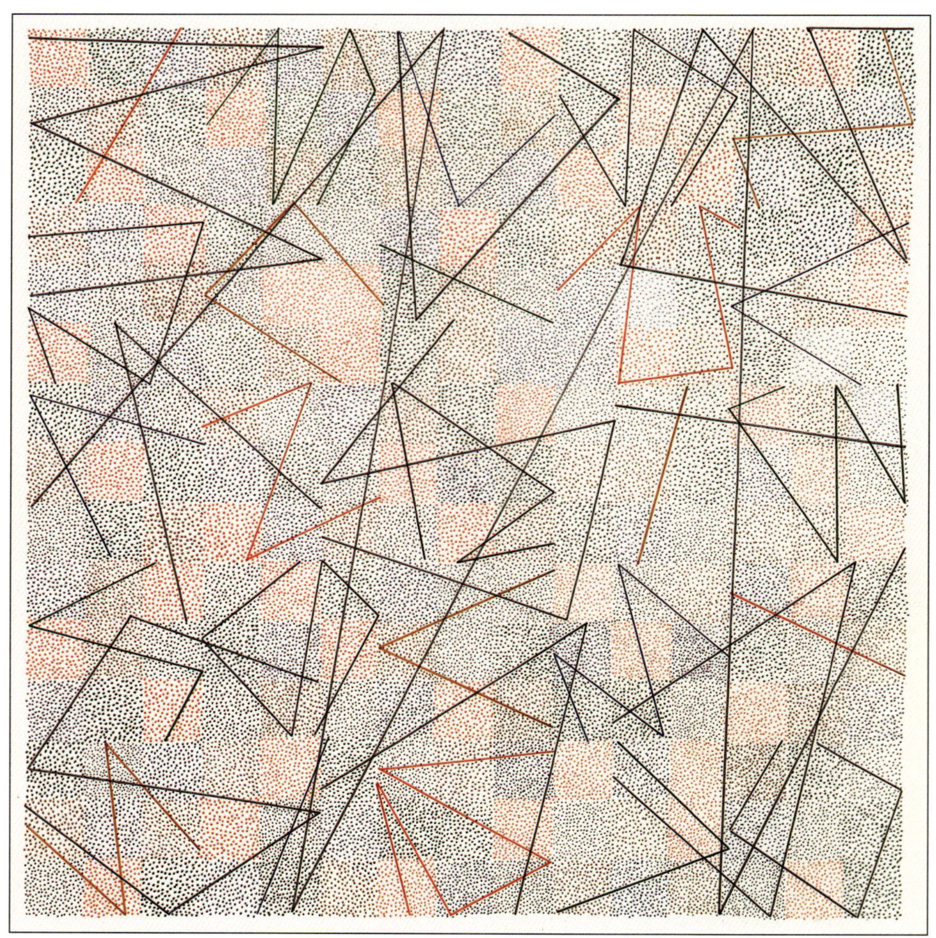

Ogham Drawings: Angled Vowels at Three Scales, 1975
Colored inks on paper, 23 x 29 in.
Collection of the artist

Dotworks: For Malevitch Even Though . . ., 1977
Colored ink on paper, 23 x 28 7/8 in.
Collection of Renato Danese

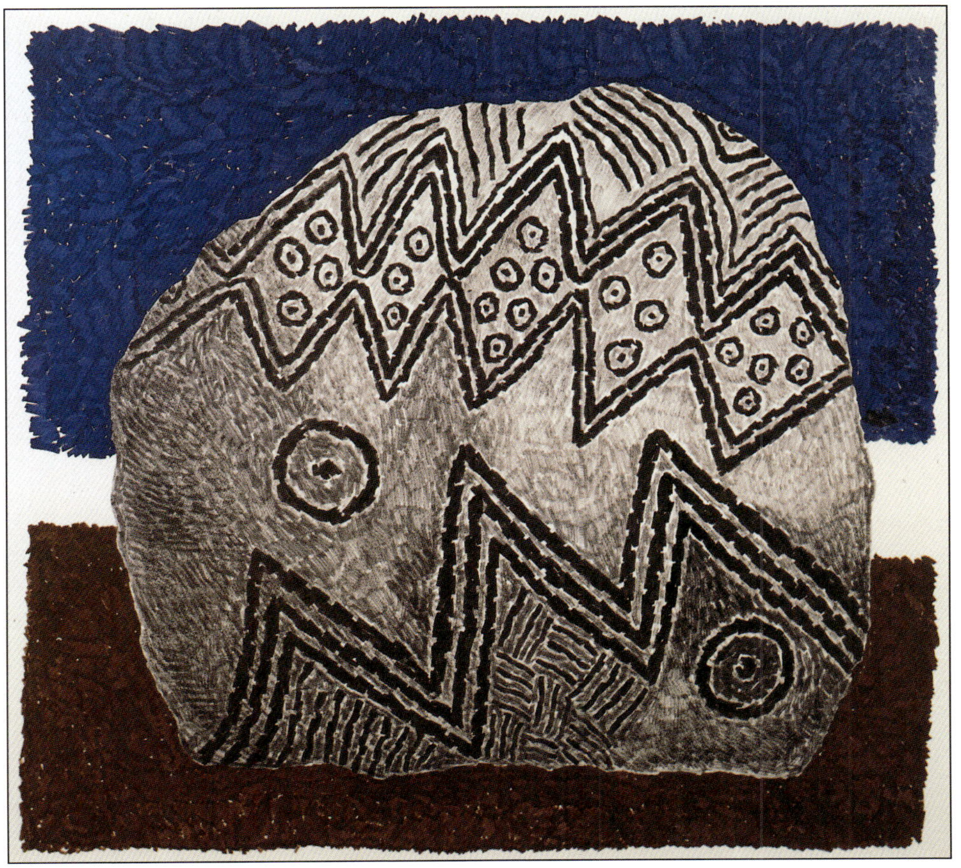

Stones: Zigzag Stone, 1983
Watercolor on paper, 45 x 47 in.
Harry and Margaret P. Glicksman Endowment Fund, Cyril W. Nave Endowment Fund, Alice Drews Gladfelter Memorial Fund purchase, 1992.334.

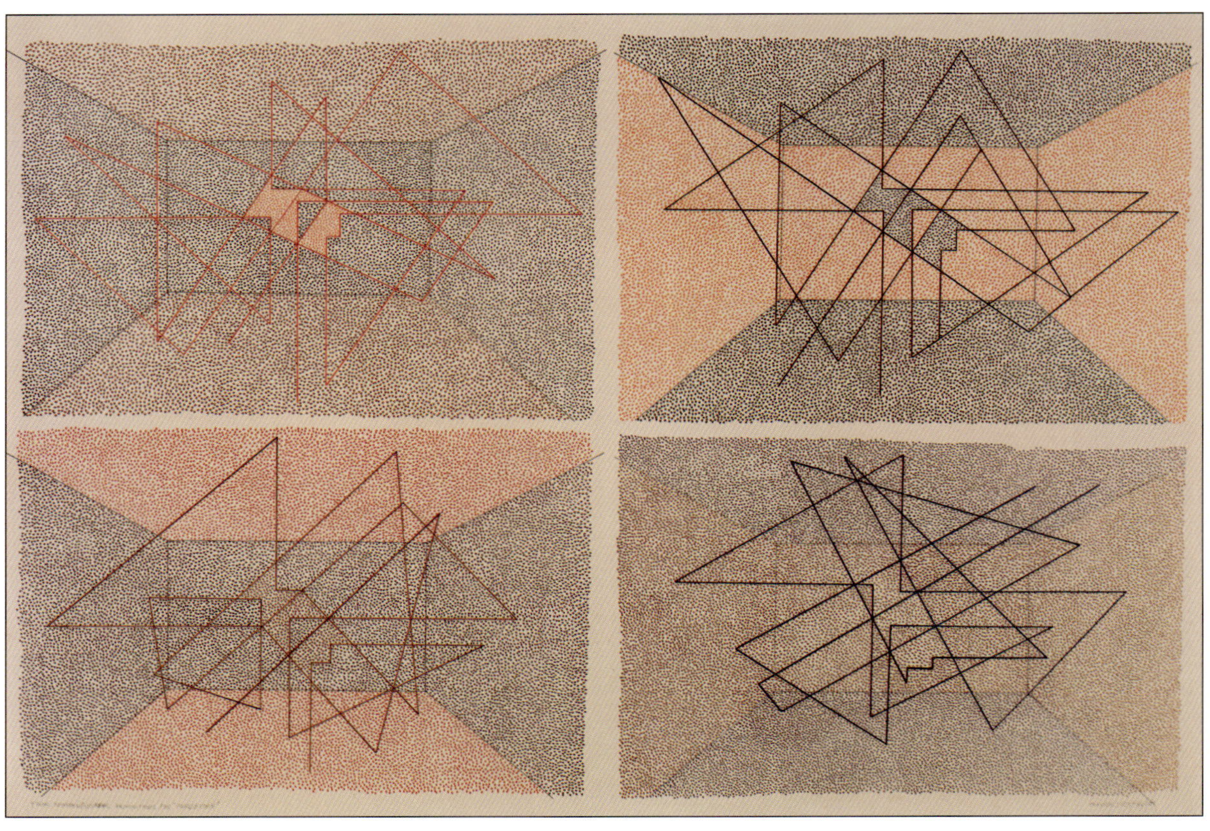

Rope Drawings: Study for the Purgatory of Humphrey Chimpden Earwicker, Homunculus, Four Spatial /Verbal Propositions, Rope Drawing #73 at the Hyde Gallery, Trinity College, Dublin, February, 1985
Colored inks on paper, 26 x 40 in.
John S. Lord Endowment Fund, Earl O. Vits Endowment Fund, Carolyn T. Anderson Endowment Fund, Walter J. and Cecille Hunt Endowment Fund purchase, 1992.333.

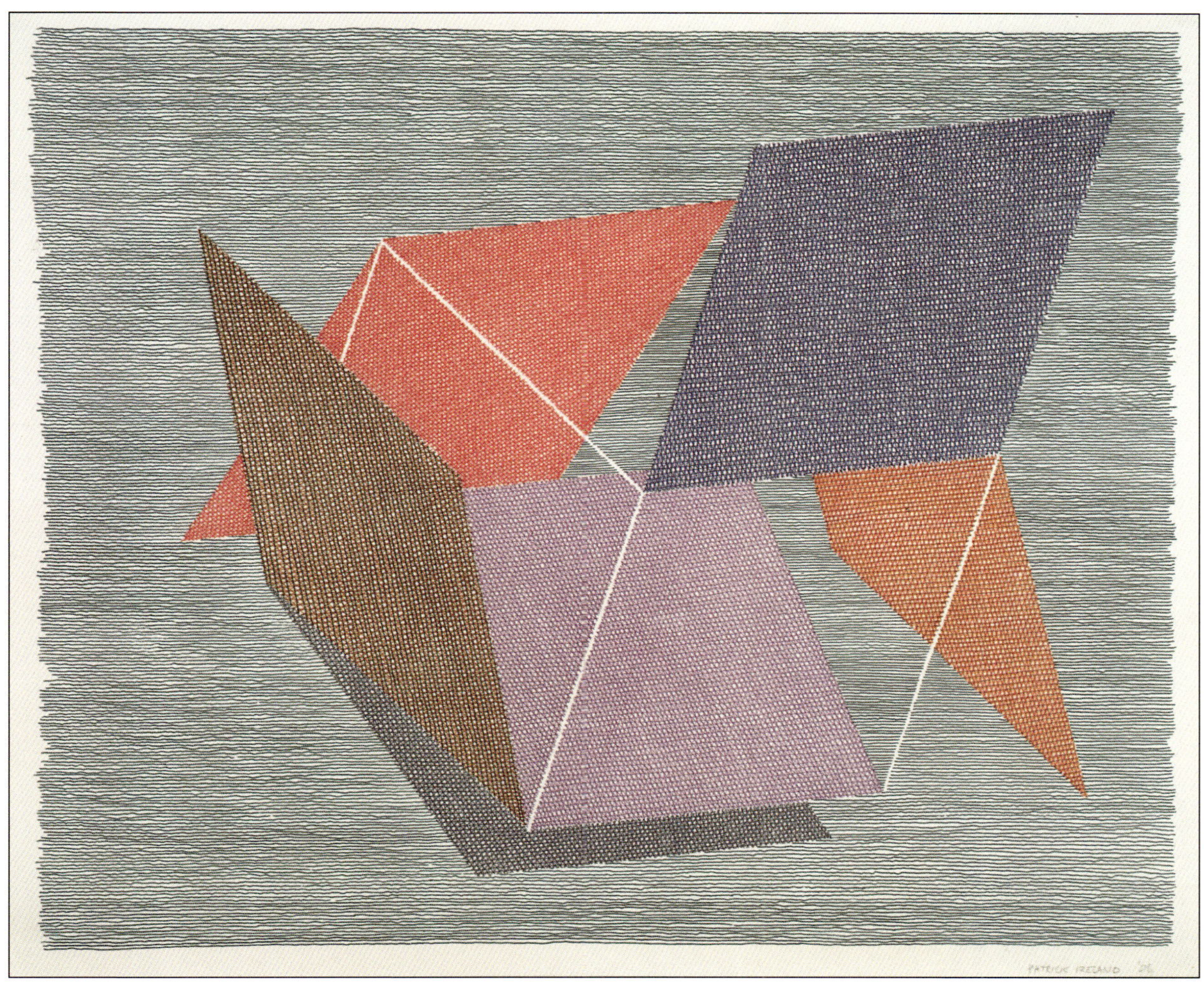

Open Box Series: Open Box on Green Ground, 1986
Colored inks on paper, 23 x 29 in.
Collection of Barbara Novak

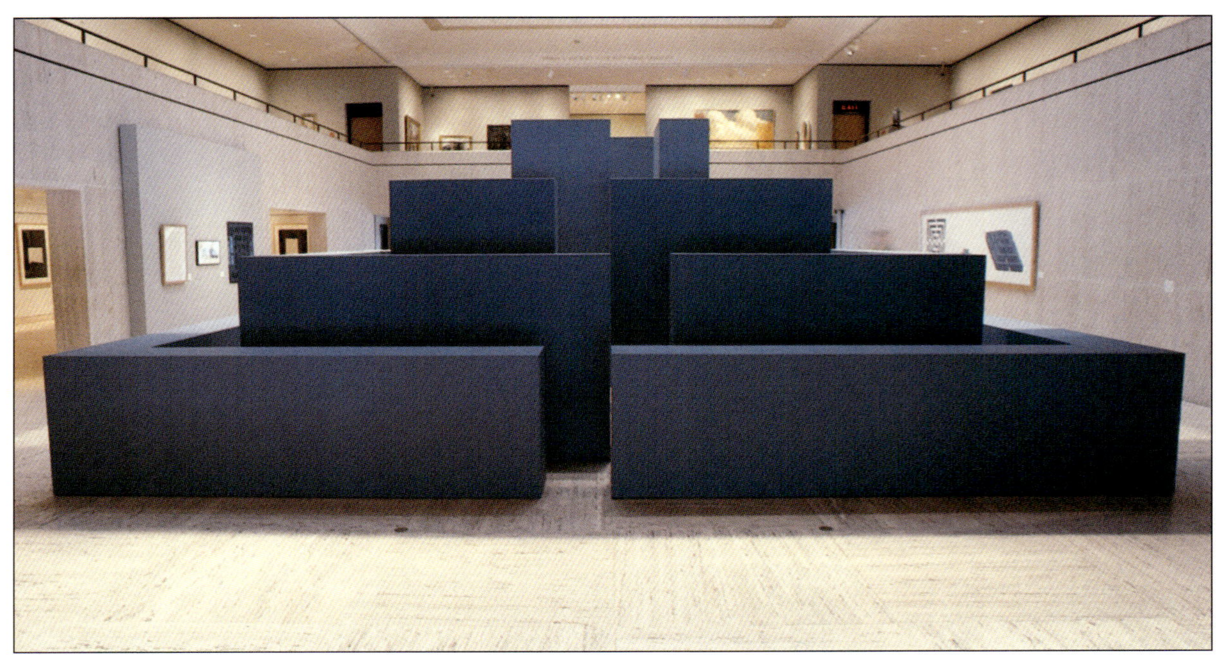

Labyrinths: Elvehjem Labyrinth, [north face, eye level] November 13, 1992—July 1, 1993
Wood, drywall installation, Paige Court of the Elvehjem Museum of Art, 9 x 24 x 24 ft.
Constructed by Tim Coughlin, John Herman, Bruce Marble, Jerry Niesen, Joe Reitmair, and Ray Wahl of the Univesity of Wisconsin–Madison's Physical Plant

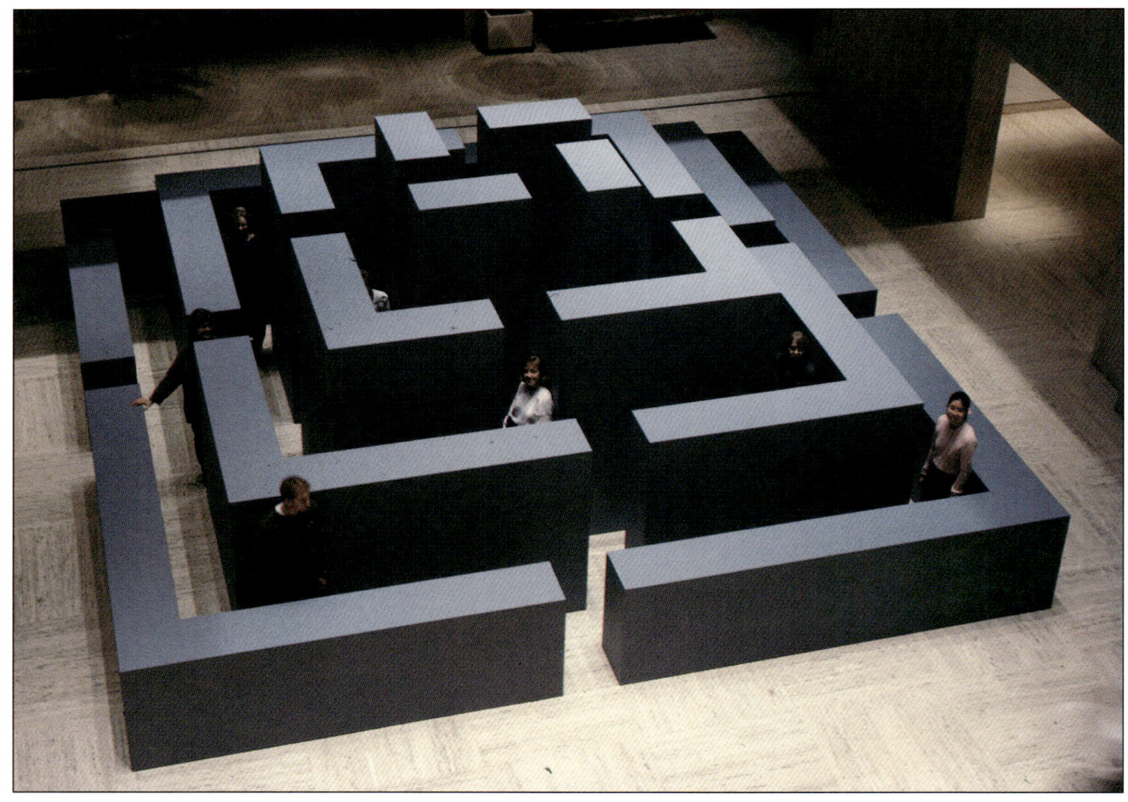

Labyrinths: Elvehjem Labyrinth, [diagonally down from southeast] November 13, 1992—July 1, 1993
Wood, drywall installation, Paige Court of the Elvehjem Museum of Art, 9 x 24 x 24 ft.

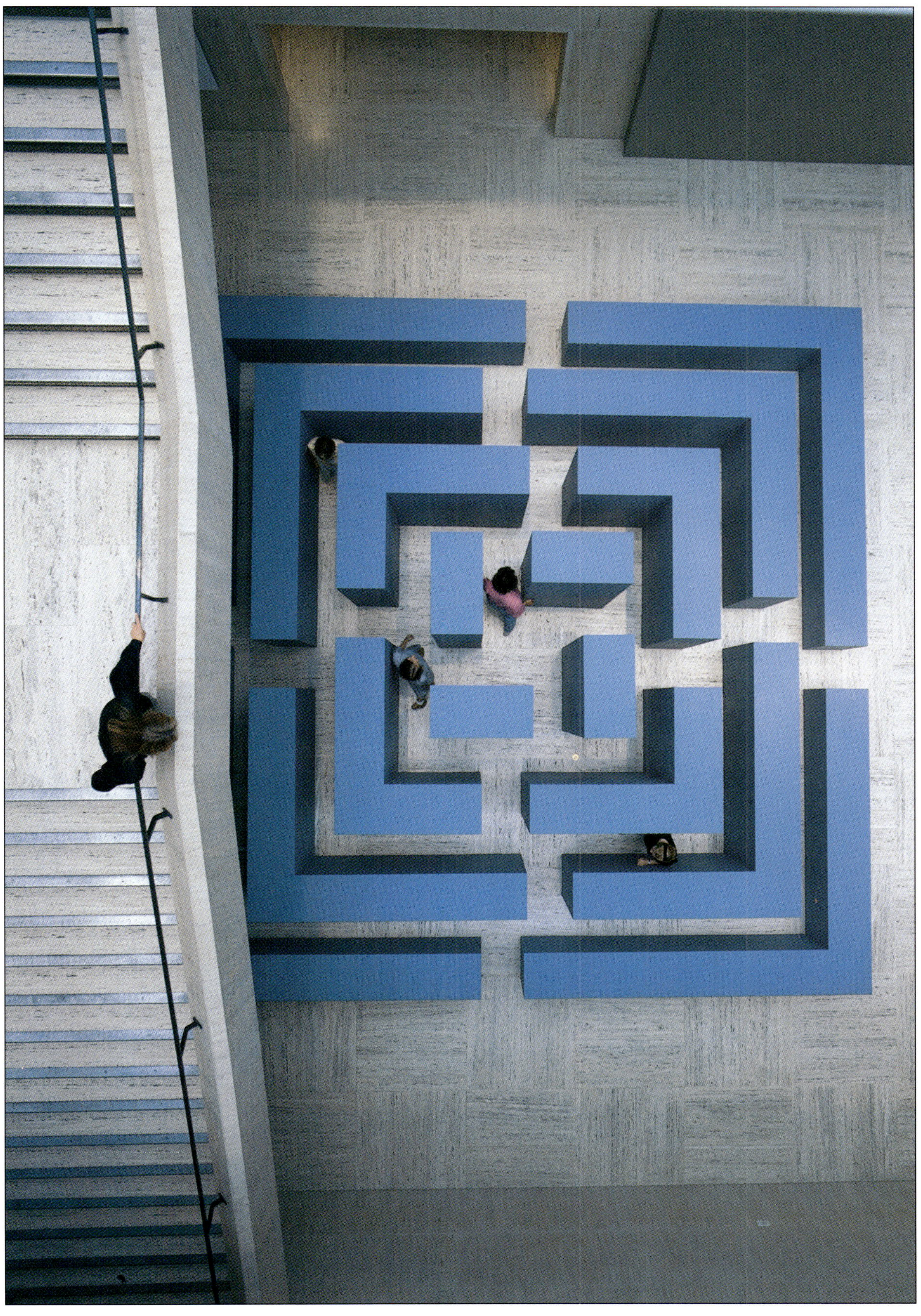

Labyrinths: Elvehjem Labyrinth, [direct overhead view] November 13, 1992—July 1, 1993
Wood, drywall installation, Paige Court of the Elvehjem Museum of Art, 9 x 24 x 24 ft.

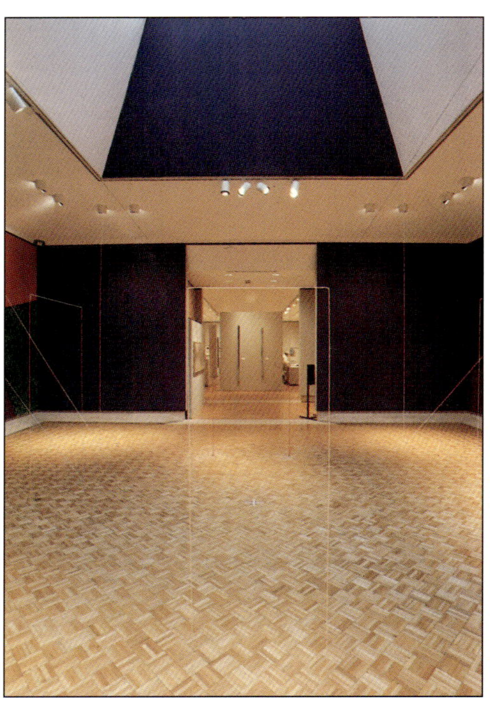

Rope Drawings: Omphalos
[north wall, looking back at entrance]
Rope Installation
November 13, 1992–January 10, 1993
Brittingham Gallery VIII, Elvehjem Museum of Art, Madison with assistance of Bruce Conover and Rick Hards

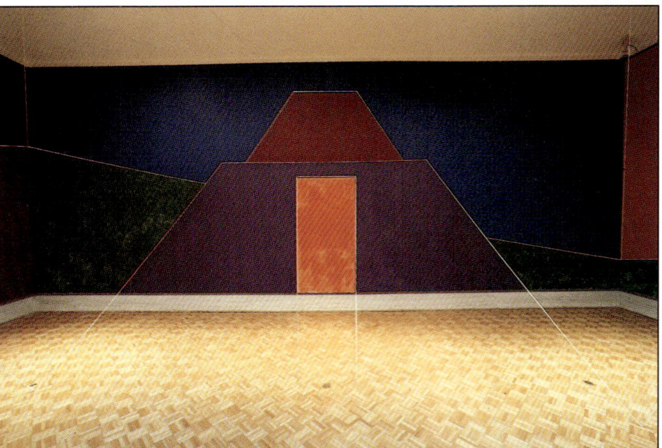

Rope Drawings: Omphalos, [south wall from central viewpoint]
Rope Installation, November 13, 1992–January 10, 1993

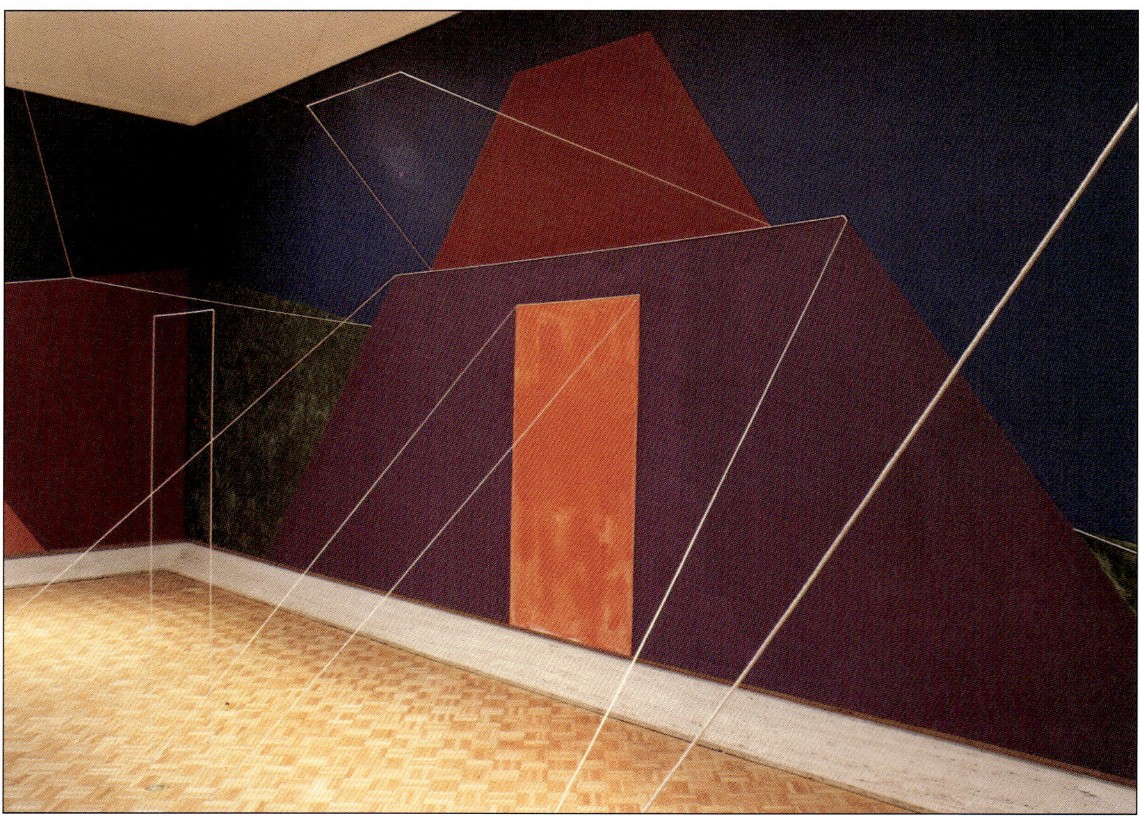

Rope Drawings: Omphalos, [south wall from angle]
Rope Installation, November 13, 1992–January 10, 1993

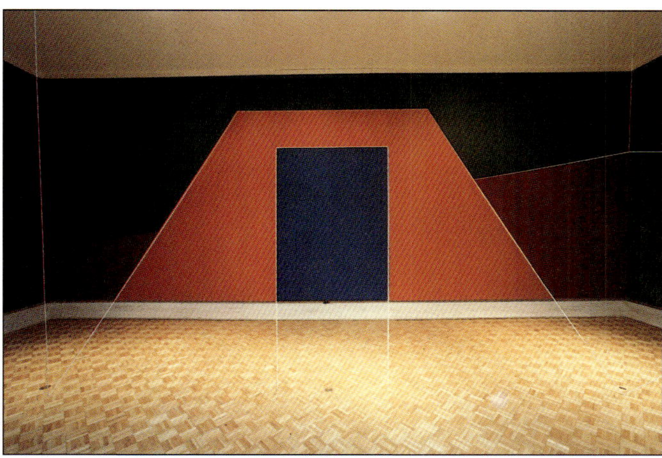

Rope Drawings: Omphalos
[east wall from central viewpoint]
Rope Installation
November 13, 1992–January 10, 1993

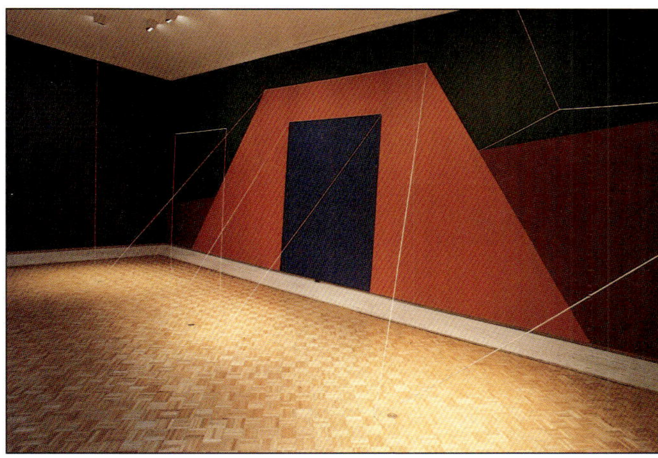

Rope Drawings: Omphalos
[east wall from angle]
Rope Installation
November 13, 1992–January 10, 1993

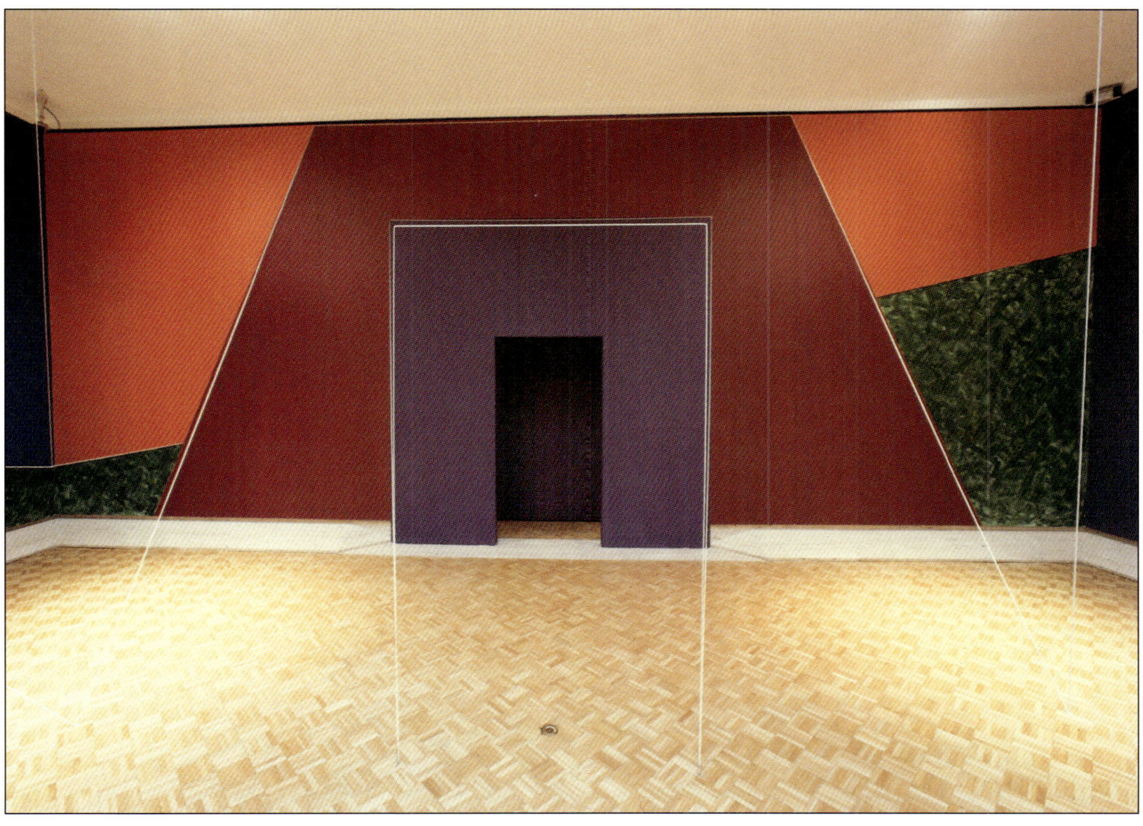

Rope Drawings: Omphalos, [west wall from central viewpoint]
Rope Installation, November 13, 1992–January 10, 1993

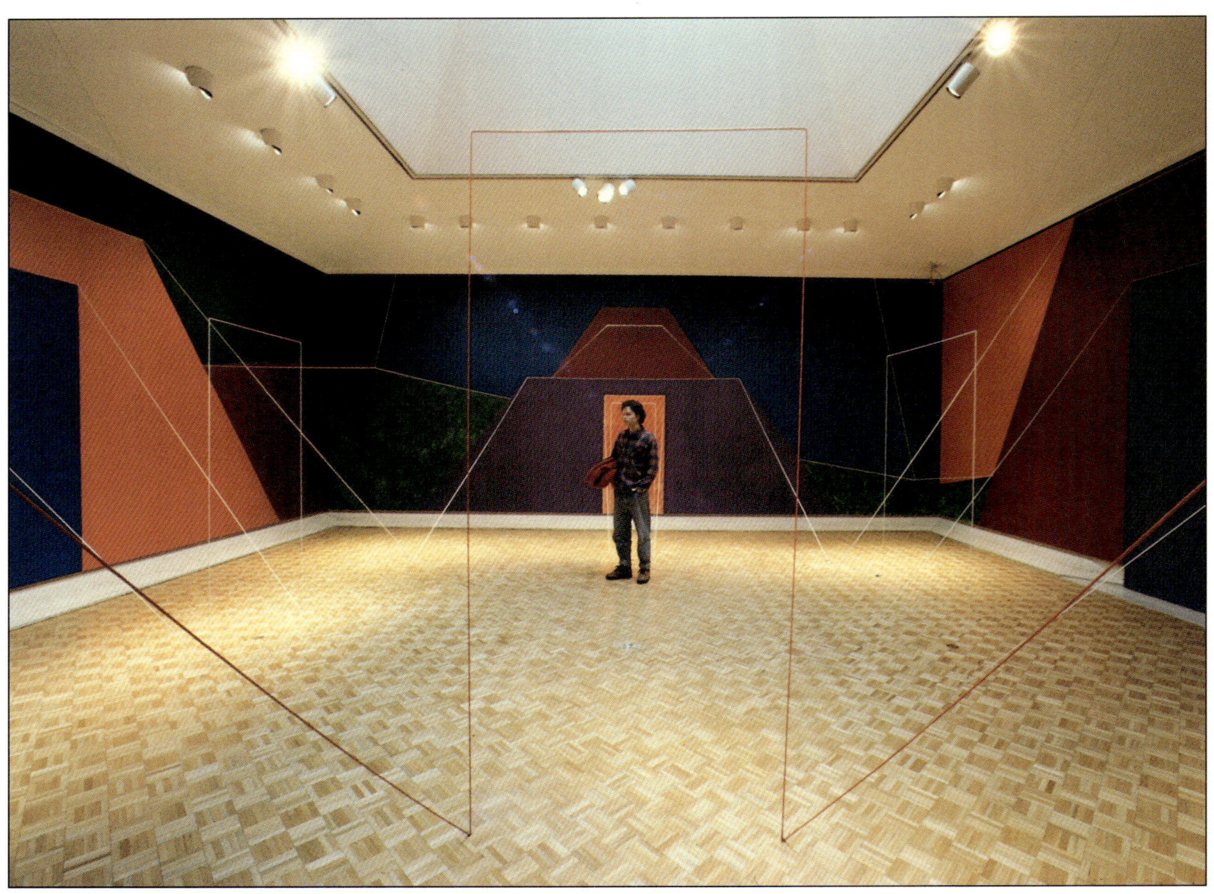

Rope Drawings: Omphalos, [overhead from north entrance]
Rope Installation, November 13, 1992–January 10, 1993

ARTIST'S CATEGORIES

GESTURES (1957–80)

CHESS SERIES (1965–67)

THE FIVE SENSES (1965–72)

WORD WORKS (Beginning 1964)

OGHAM DRAWINGS (Beginning 1967)

OGHAM SCULPTURES (1967–71)

"I" DRAWINGS (Beginning 1969)

DOTWORKS (Beginning 1970)

ARTIST'S BOOKS (Beginning 1966)

OPEN BOX SERIES (Beginning 1975)

FOYERS AND WELLS (1967–69)

LABYRINTHS (1967–68, 1992)

ROPE DRAWINGS (Beginning 1972)

STONES (1982–84)

CHECKLIST

BY ARTIST'S CATEGORIES

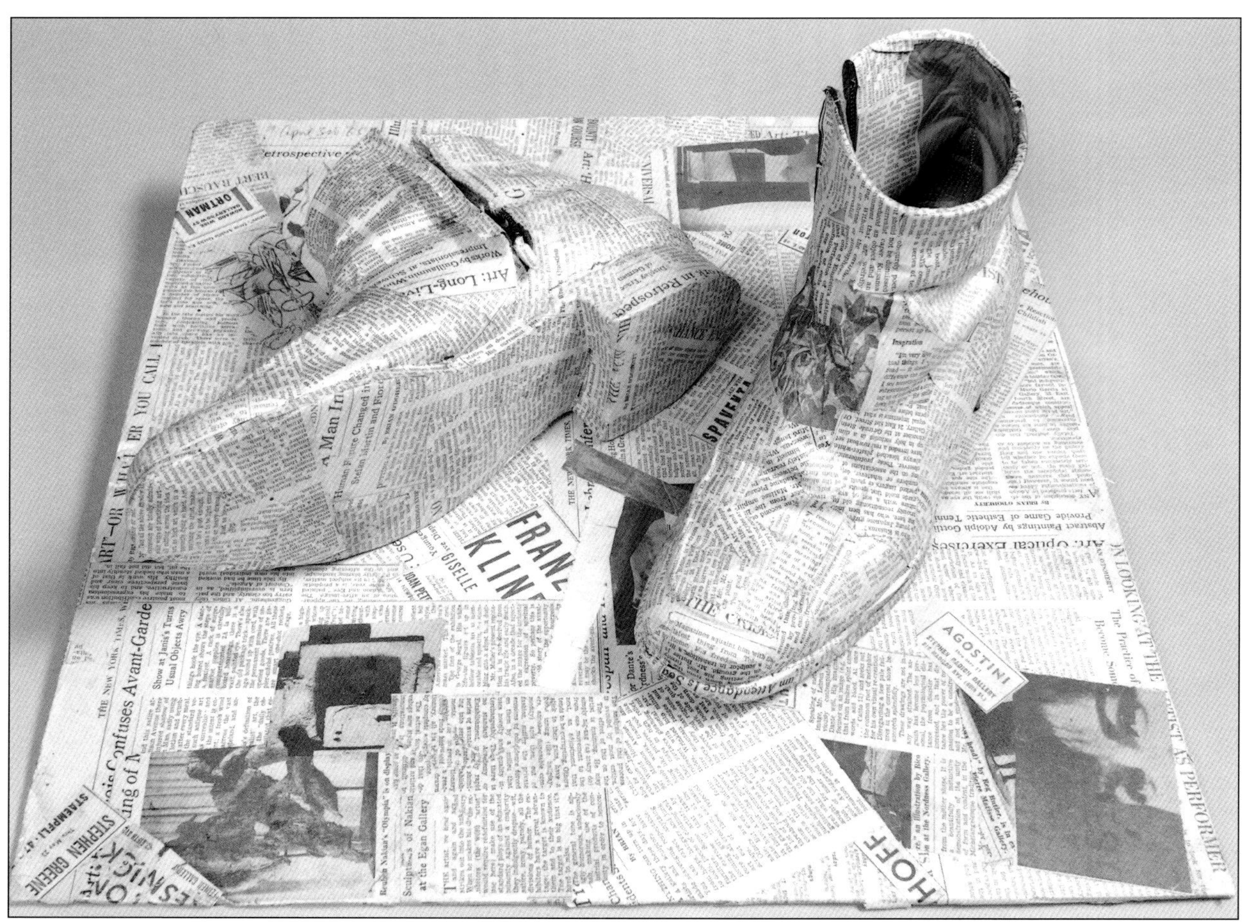

The Critic's Boots, 1964-65
Leather, newspaper, base: 18 x18 in.; boot size 10
Collection of the artist

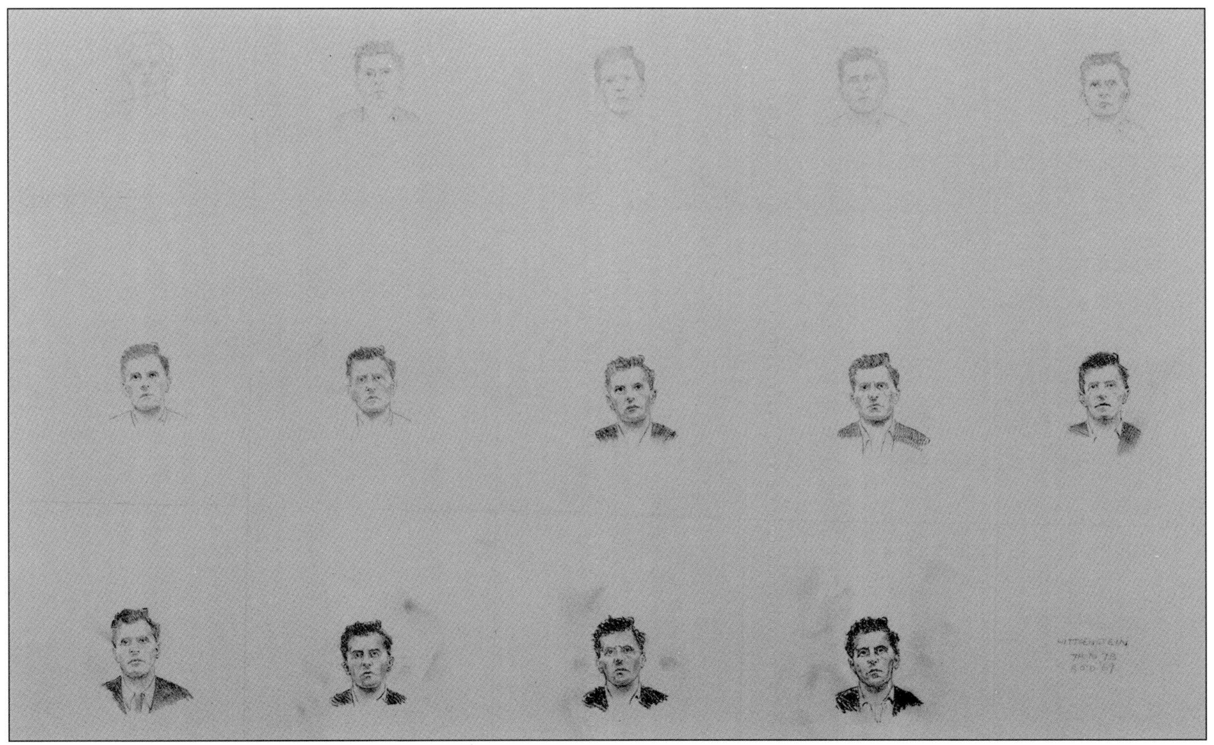

Wittgenstein 7H to 7B, 1967
Pencil on paper, 21 x 29 in.
Collection of the artist

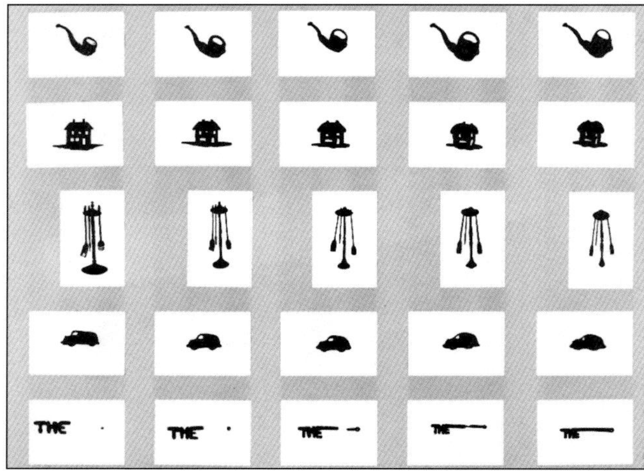

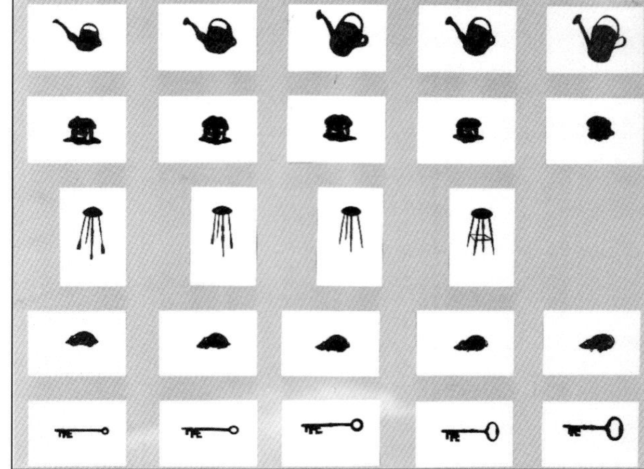

Between Categories, 1957–68
Handwritten and typed text on paper and ink on paper, drawings on paper collaged onto posterboard, each board approx. 30 x 40 in.
Collection of the artist

P E R C E P T I O N

Stimulus - Selective Mechanism ATTENDING
Integrating Mechanism PERCEIVING = meaningful patterns from cues

ATTENDING Some facts: Eyes spans 180"
Central Foveal area 2"
The eye is virtually blind when in motion.

Attention invloves selection and conversely elimination. Obviously all stimuli cannot be dealt with equally.

Attention is composed of physical set and mental set, or expectancy, or pre-perc.

Basic to both is motivation : Drives determine the direction of attention. Attention is a function of the entire organism.

Eye movements and the 'Constant Shifting of Attention'. Due to fatigueing of sensory cells in the retina. Seems to be a device for maintaining the stimulus. EG ambiguous figures, and the shift between two perceptions.

External factors in Attention Shift:
A stimulus attracts attention by its INTENSITY
CONTRAST
NOVELTY
MOVEMENT OR CHANGE
SIZE
REPETITION OR SUMMATION OF WEAK STIM
OCCASIONALLY DURATION

This is involuntary attention dominated by external stimuli.

Also a form of attending which is controlled by internal conditions.
or
Internal conditions producing motivation = voluntary attention.

Voluntary attention can become habitual, that is involuntary but the point of distinction is that it was once voluntary.

Attention involves muscular tension. Attending is the device by which we exclude irrelevant stimuli the more effectively to deal with those of importance to the motives of the moment.

A persisting mental set interferes with attention to objects outside its scope.

ATTENTION IS THE PROCESS BY WHICH STIMULI GAIN CLARITY. IT IS STIMULUS SELECTION at a given moment the organism is related to a particular stimulus and excludes others from consideration.
CONSEQUENCE = Clearness of perception and muscular adjustment.

Between Categories (Detail)

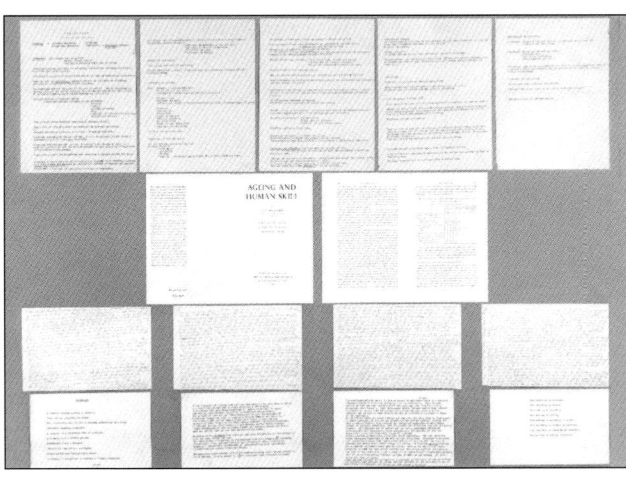

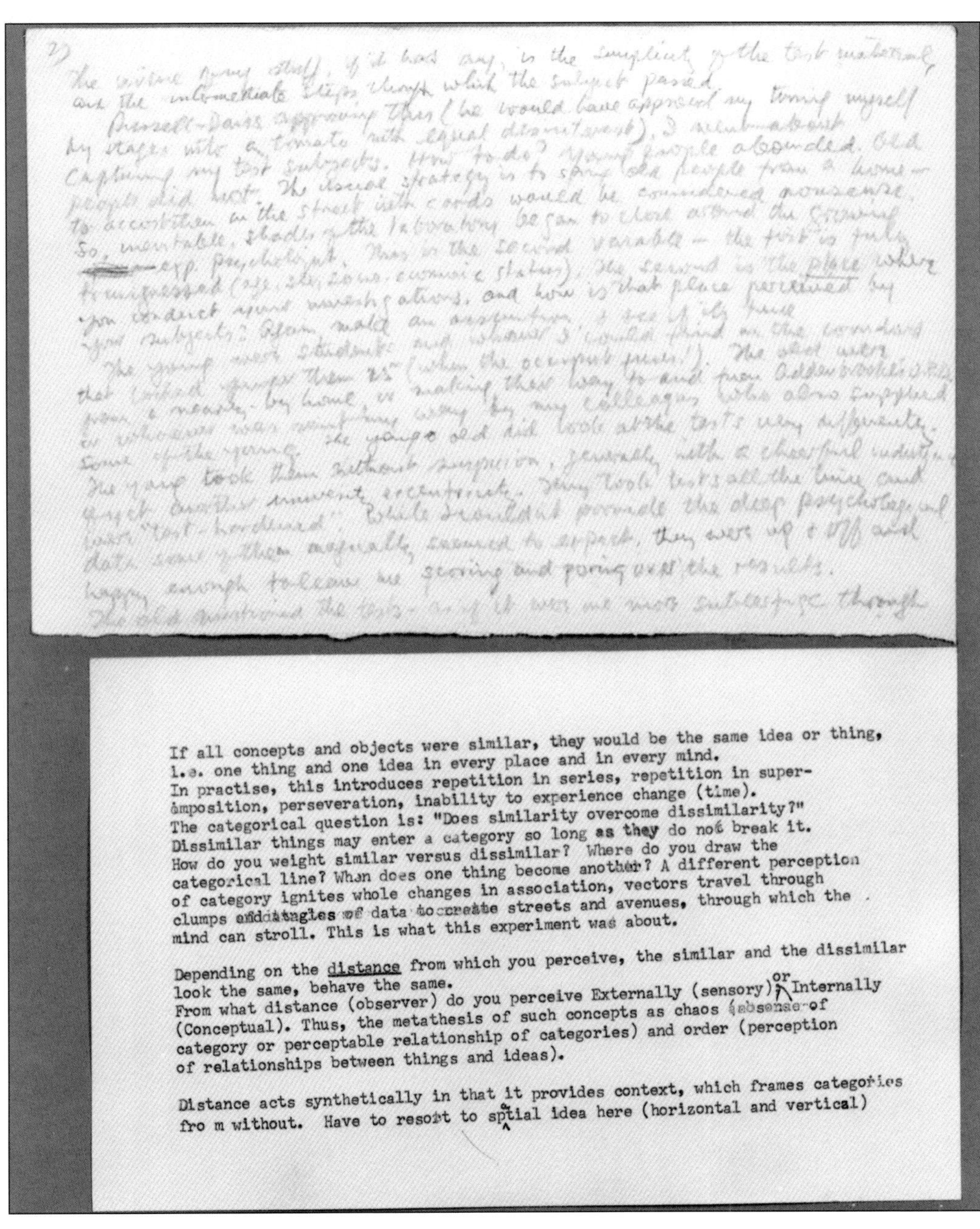

If all concepts and objects were similar, they would be the same idea or thing,
i.e. one thing and one idea in every place and in every mind.
In practise, this introduces repetition in series, repetition in super-
imposition, perseveration, inability to experience change (time).
The categorical question is: "Does similarity overcome dissimilarity?"
Dissimilar things may enter a category so long as they do not break it.
How do you weight similar versus dissimilar? Where do you draw the
categorical line? When does one thing become another? A different perception
of category ignites whole changes in association, vectors travel through
clumps and tangles of data to create streets and avenues, through which the
mind can stroll. This is what this experiment was about.

Depending on the distance from which you perceive, the similar and the dissimilar
look the same, behave the same.
From what distance (observer) do you perceive Externally (sensory) or Internally
(Conceptual). Thus, the metathesis of such concepts as chaos (absense of
category or perceptable relationship of categories) and order (perception
of relationships between things and ideas).

Distance acts synthetically in that it provides context, which frames categories
fro m without. Have to resort to spatial idea here (horizontal and vertical)

Between Categories (Detail)

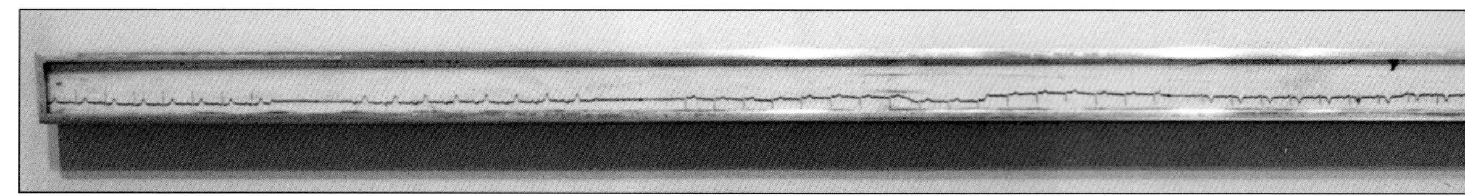

Portrait of Marcel Duchamp: Uncut Cardiogram, 1966
Ink on paper, 1½ x 95½ in.
Collection of the artist

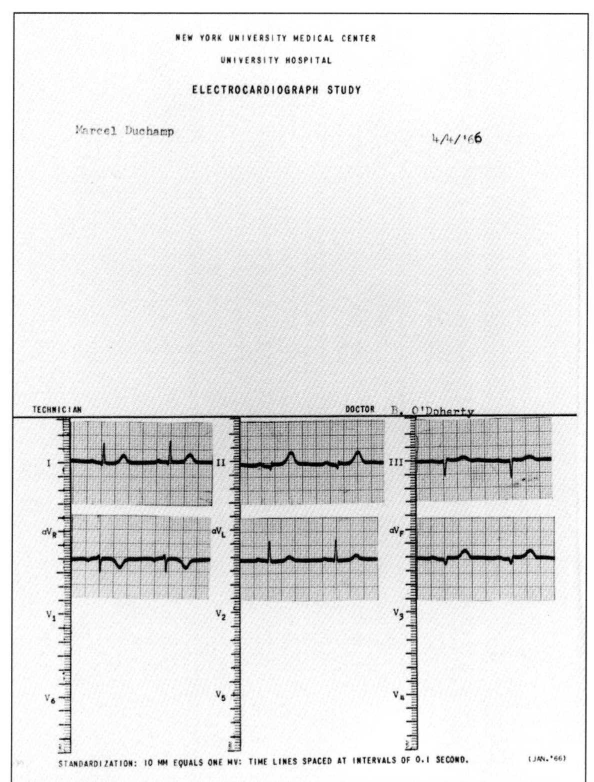

NEW YORK UNIVERSITY MEDICAL CENTER
UNIVERSITY HOSPITAL
ELECTROCARDIOGRAPH STUDY

Marcel Duchamp 4/4/'66

TECHNICIAN DOCTOR B. O'Doherty

I II III
aV_R aV_L aV_F
V_1 V_2 V_3
V_6 V_5 V_4

STANDARDIZATION: 10 MM EQUALS ONE MV: TIME LINES SPACED AT INTERVALS OF 0.1 SECOND. (JAN.'66)

Portrait of Marcel Duchamp: Mounted Cardiogram, 4/4/66
Ink and typewriter on paper, 11 x 8½ in.
Collection of the artist

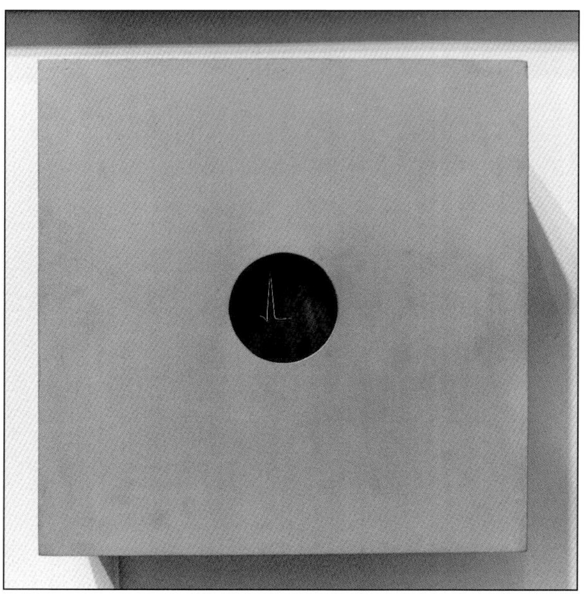

Portrait of Marcel Duchamp: Slow Pulse Rate, 1966
Mixed media, 16⅝ x 16⅝ x 8 in.
Collecion of the artist

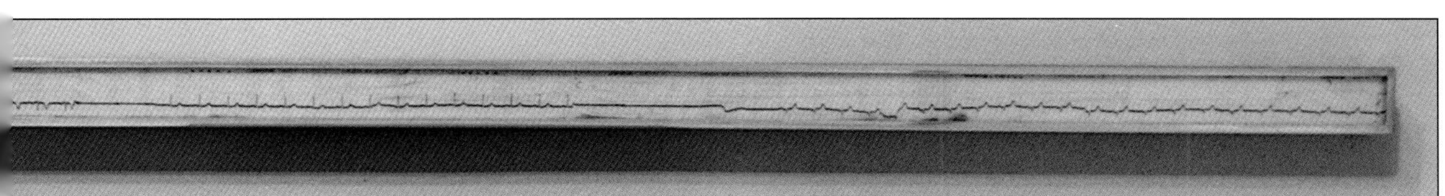

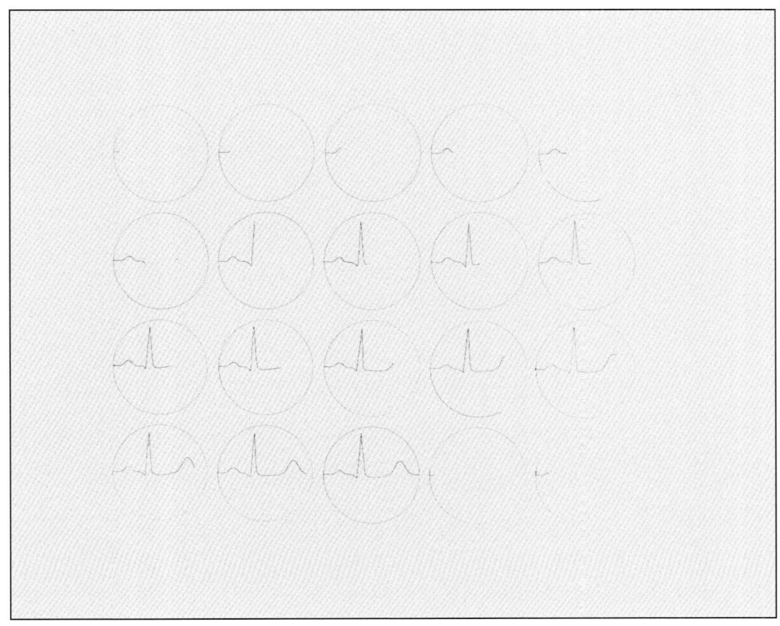

Study for Second Portrait of Marcel Duchamp: Lead One, Mounting Increments, 1967
Ink on paper, 23 x 29 in.
Collection of the artist

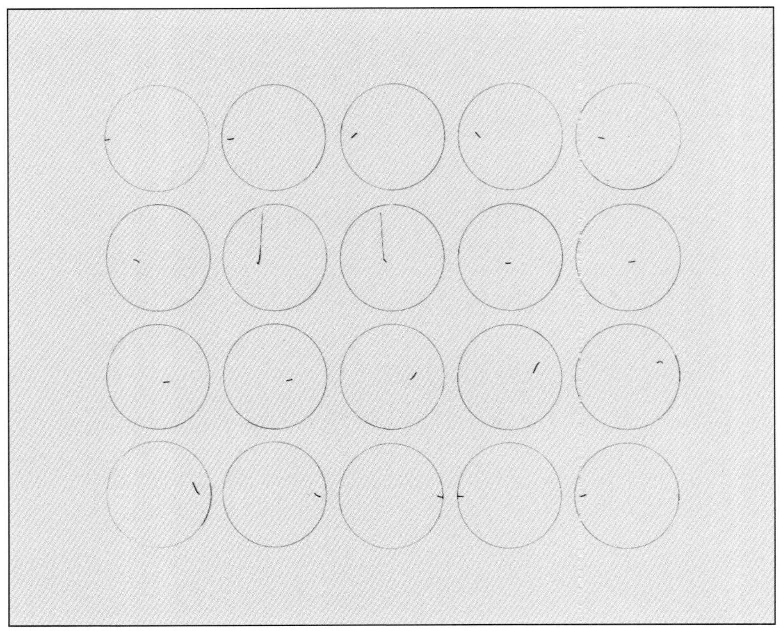

Study for Second Portrait of Marcel Duchamp: Lead One, Isolated Increments, 1967
Ink on paper, 23 x 29 in.
Collection of the artist

ON THE WAY HOME FROM SCHOOL, HE STOPPED IN FRONT OF AN EMPTY SHOP WINDOW. THE GLASS DOORWAY WAS RECESSED FROM THE STREET. FROM EITHER SIDE OF IT, TWO WINDOWS, LIKE GLASSY WINGS, MOVED OUT AT AN ANGLE TOWARDS THE LINE OF STOREFRONTS, MAKING, IN SECTION, A FLAT V WITH A SHORT HORIZONTAL BASE.

STANDING OPPOSITE THE DOOR, HE FOUND HIS THREE REFLECTIONS LIKE SENTINELS IN DOOR AND WINDOWS. THE WINDOWS REFLECTED IN REVERSE THE SIGNS ACROSS THE STREET BEHIND HIM: SHADES/ FOR TABLES/CHANDELIERS/LAMPS CHAN/COMPLETE LINE/COCA-COLA/BURGERLAND. ON THE RIGHT-HAND WINDOW, UNREVERSED, WAS A LARGE RED FOR RENT SIGN. HE HEARD THE SOUND OF THE TRAFFIC PASS BEHIND HIM FROM LEFT TO RIGHT. BEFORE HIM, THE NOISELESS SIMULACRA OF LORRY, VAN, BUS, CAR JUMPED ODDLY ACROSS GLASS.

WITHIN THE EMPTY SHOP, DIM UNREFLECTED OBJECTS SHOWED OCCASIONAL HIGHLIGHTS LIKE DISTANT STARS. WHEN HE MOVED, THE GIANT CRYSTAL OF THE SHOPFRONT ABRUPTLY SHATTERED INTO A WILDERNESS OF REFLECTIONS.

TWO PAIRS OF LONG NEON TUBES IN THE CEILING REPLICATED THE INCLINE OF THE WINDOWS.

BEYOND HIS REFLECTION IN THE DOOR, INDEED INSIDE HIS REFLECTION, AS IN A BLOCK OF ICE, A TINY SIMULACRUM OF HIMSELF WAS VISIBLE IN A DISTANT MIRROR ON THE BACK WALL OF THE STORE. BOTH REFLECTIONS MIMICED HIS MOVES, THOUGH THE FAR IMAGE SEEMED TO RESPOND WITH A SLIGHT DELAY.

PEDESTRIANS PASSED BETWEEN HIM AND THE SHOP; THE STREAM OF TRAFFIC PASSED NOISILY BEHIND HIM. IN FRONT OF HIM, THE REFLECTED CARS MIGHT HAVE BEEN LUMPS OF MATTER SUMMONED TO DISPLAY AN EXTRAORDINARY WRINKLE IN THE LOGIC OF THE WORLD.

AS THE ~~REFLECTED~~ TRAFFIC PASSED BEHIND HIM FROM LEFT TO RIGHT ON THE ONE-WAY STREET, IT APPEARED FIRST IN THE RIGHT-HAND WINDOW, THEN FLASHED ACROSS THE GLASS DOOR, THEN APPEARED IN THE LEFT-HAND WINDOW.

THE WHITE VAN IN THE RIGHT-HAND WINDOW WAS JUST BEGINNING TO ARRIVE IN THE CENTER DOOR WHILE SIMULTANEOUSLY BEGINNING ITS DEPARTURE IN THE LEFT-HAND WINDOW, WHERE IT WAS MOMENTARILY DETAINED BY THE GILLS OF A RADIATOR BEHIND THE GLASS. A BLUE TRUCK ON THE RIGHT, COVERED WITH A BLACK TARPAULIN, REMAINED PARKED IN THE FUTURE. ON THE LEFT, A BLUE-TOPPED VAN, WITH A DOUBLE REAR WINDOW, UNREFLECTED ELSEWHERE, WAS DEPARTING FARTHER INTO THE PAST. THE NORMAL SEQUENCE OF THE TRAFFIC ON THE STREET BEHIND HIM WAS THUS REVERSED IN THE GLASS FROM 1-2-3 TO 3-2-1.

THIS HIATUS IN LOGIC WAS DUE TO THE INCLINATION OF THE WINDOWS. BUT THIS DISTURBANCE IN SEQUENCE WAS, MORE IMPORTANTLY, A DISTURBANCE IN TIME.

EACH DAY, ON HIS WAY BACK FROM SCHOOL, HE READ THE REFLECTIONS IN WINDOWS AND DOOR WITH INCREASING SKILL. THE REVERSAL OF THE TRAFFIC FLOW WAS EXPERIENCED BY HIS THREE REFLECTED IMAGES, EACH IMPRISONED IN ITS OWN WINDOW, AS A REVERSAL OF HIS OWN FUTURE AND PAST. SOMEWHERE, IF HE COULD FIND IT, THE SHOP WINDOW WAS OFFERING HIM A FLAW IN TIME, AN OBLIQUE PLANE THROUGH WHICH HE MIGHT SLIP INTO THE THREE GLASS PLANES THAT REVERSED TIME AND ITS TENSES.

SINCE HIS NOTION OF TIME WAS UNSTABLE, HE SEEMED TO BE REMEMBERING THE FUTURE (THE RIGHT-HAND WINDOW) AND FORESTALLING THE PAST (THE LEFT HAND WINDOW). AGAIN AND AGAIN, WHAT HE SAW ON THE RIGHT JUMPED BACK TO PASS THROUGH THE GLASS DOOR. WHAT HE SAW ON THE LEFT HAD ALREADY PASSED.

FEELING HIMSELF SLIPPING BACK AND FORTH IN TIME, LOSING HIS FOOTING IN THE SECULAR WORLD, THE SPIRITUAL COORDINATES IN WHICH HE HAD BEEN REARED PRESSED UPON HIM. HE DID NOT KNOW WHEN THE THREE PANES OF GLASS, REPRESENTING THREE TIMES, BECAME THE Three Persons. God the Father, THE JUDGEMENT THAT AWAITED, WAS IN THE WINDOW ON THE RIGHT, WAITING FOR THE PRESENT TO CATCH UP WITH Him. THE Son, His SACRIFICE IN THE PAST, WAS IN THE WINDOW ON THE LEFT. BUT WHERE WAS THE Holy Ghost? HE WAS RARELY SEEN, EXCEPT AS A DOVE, OR RAYS OF LIGHT AND ON ONE OCCASION AS TONGUES OF FIRE. HIS MOTHER PRAYED TO THE Father OF THE FUTURE AND THE Son OF THE PAST. BUT WHO COULD PRAY TO THE Holy Ghost, THE MOST ELUSIVE OF THE Three? WAS HE ONLY PRESENT IN THE CENTRAL DOOR, WHERE IMAGES TWITCHED BRIEFLY BY? THE Holy Ghost DID NOT BECOME INVOLVED IN THE TRANSACTIONS OF TERROR AND GUILT INSISTED ON BY THE Son, WHOSE INFINITE HUMILIATION HAD MADE His Father SO REVENGEFUL AND MAD. WAS THE Holy Ghost AN OBLIQUE PLANE THROUGH WHICH HE COULD SLIP INTO A GLASSY ETERNITY AWAY FROM TIME?

SHUTTLING BETWEEN HIS THREE REFLECTIONS IN THE REVERSED SPACE OF THREE TENSES, HE TRIED TO CATCH GLIMPSES OF THE Holy Ghost. THE Holy Ghost, HE DECIDED, RESIDED NOT IN THE REFLECTIONS, BUT IN THE GLASS ITSELF, FROZEN INTO His OWN ETERNITY. THE OTHER Two Persons HAD CREATED TIME, BUT THE Holy Ghost DID NOT BELIEVE IT. LOOKING AT THE SHOPFRONT, WHICH TURNED LOGIC INTO PARADOX, REVERSED FUTURE AND PAST, COMPRESSING INSIDE AND OUTSIDE AGAINST THE SAME INVISIBLE PLANES OF GLASS, HE KNEW THAT AT ANY MOMENT ANY ONE OF HIS THREE IMAGES COULD BE SNATCHED INTO A TIME OR A TENSE THAT WOULD ANNIHILATE HIM. HIS TRIPLICATED BODY WAS PERILOUSLY SUSTAINED. A SHUDDER IN THE GLASS COULD MAKE HIM FALL APART—HIS ARM MIGHT BECOME FOREIGN TO HIS LEG; ONE EYE MIGHT END UP A WEEK AWAY FROM THE OTHER. IF HE BELIEVED IN TIME, Father OR Son MIGHT FRAGMENT HIM IN AN ICY APOCALYPSE. IF HE DID NOT, THE Holy Ghost MIGHT FREEZE HIM INTO THE GLASS WHERE HE WOULD BECOME INVISIBLE TO HIMSELF, DISPERSED TO NOTHING. WHEN HE WALKED AWAY, HIS REFLECTIONS REMAINED IN THE THREE PANES OF GLASS. EACH DAY HE RETURNED TO MAKE SURE THEY WERE STILL THERE.

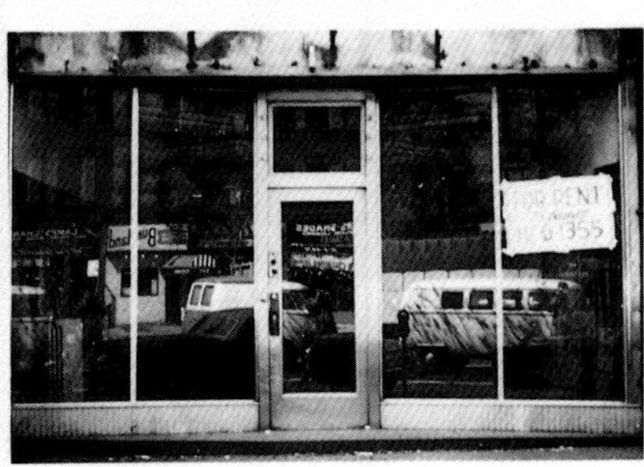

PASTPRESENTFUTURE
PASTFUTUREPRESENT
PRESENTPASTFUTURE
PRESENTFUTUREPAST
FUTUREPASTPRESENT
FUTUREPRESENTPAST

PORTRAIT OF THE ARTIST AET. 7

Past, Present, Future (Portrait of Artist Aet. 7), 1967
Photo and text on posterboard, 23 x 29 in.
Collection of the artist

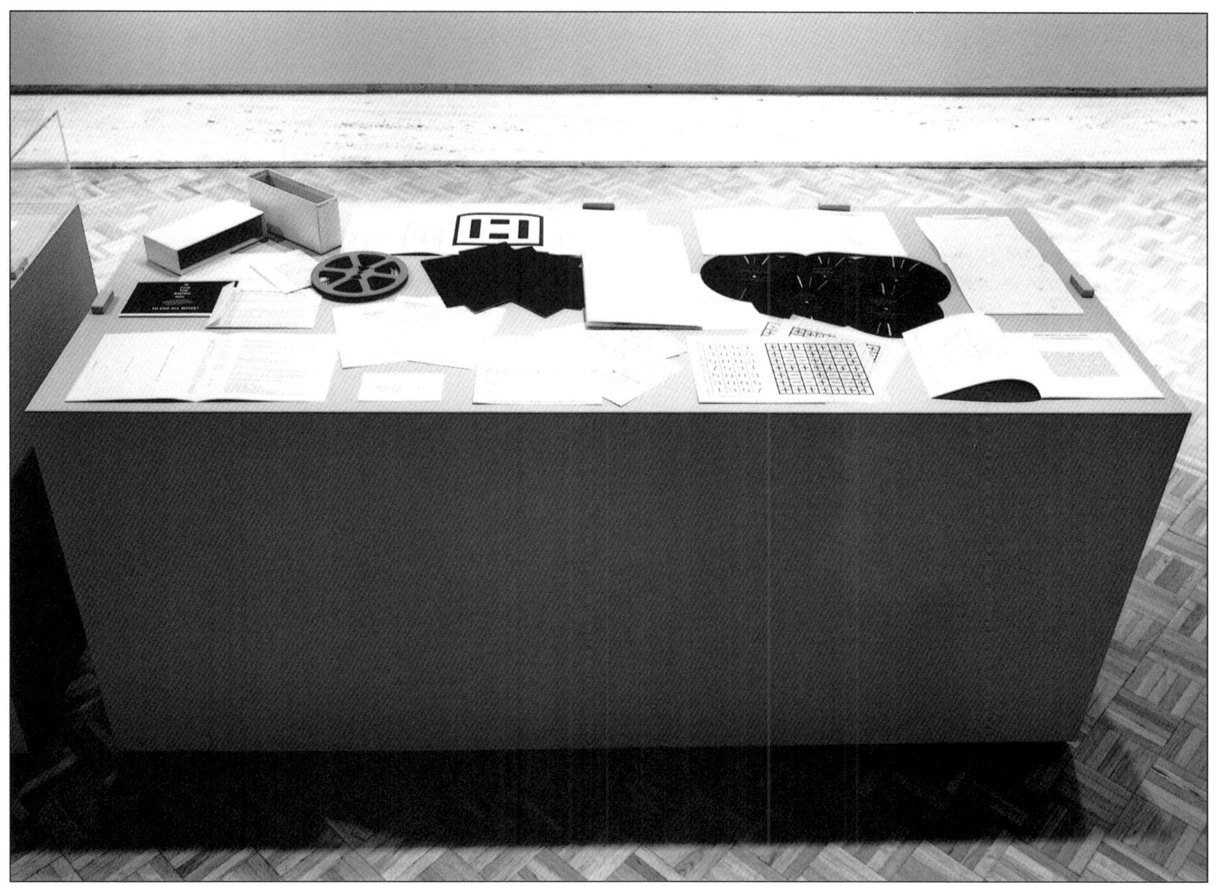

Aspen 5/6, 1967–68
Exhibition in a box, various objects in mixed media
Collection of the artist

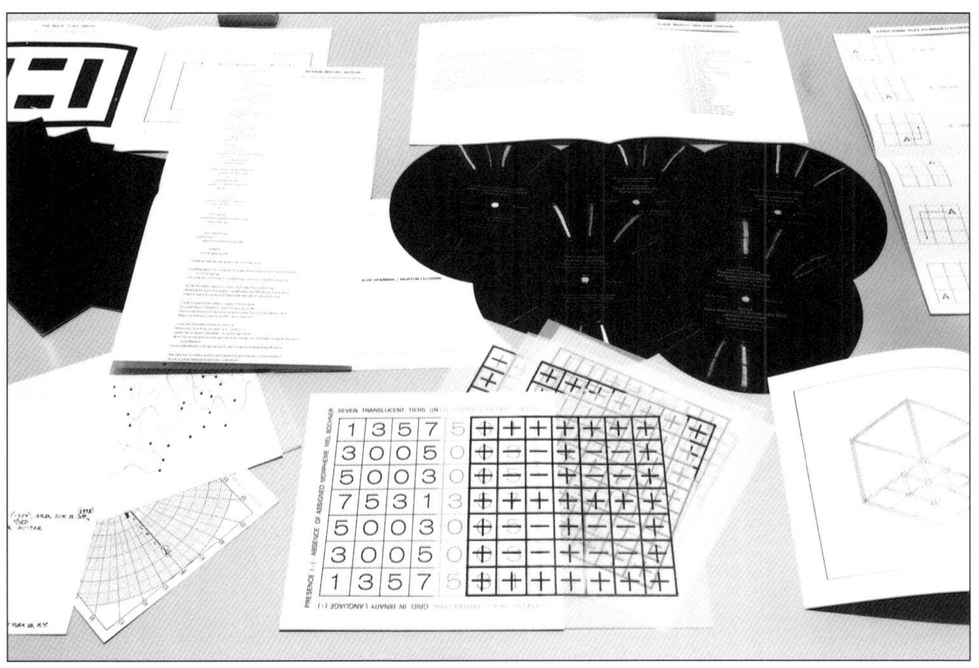

Aspen 5/6 (Detail)

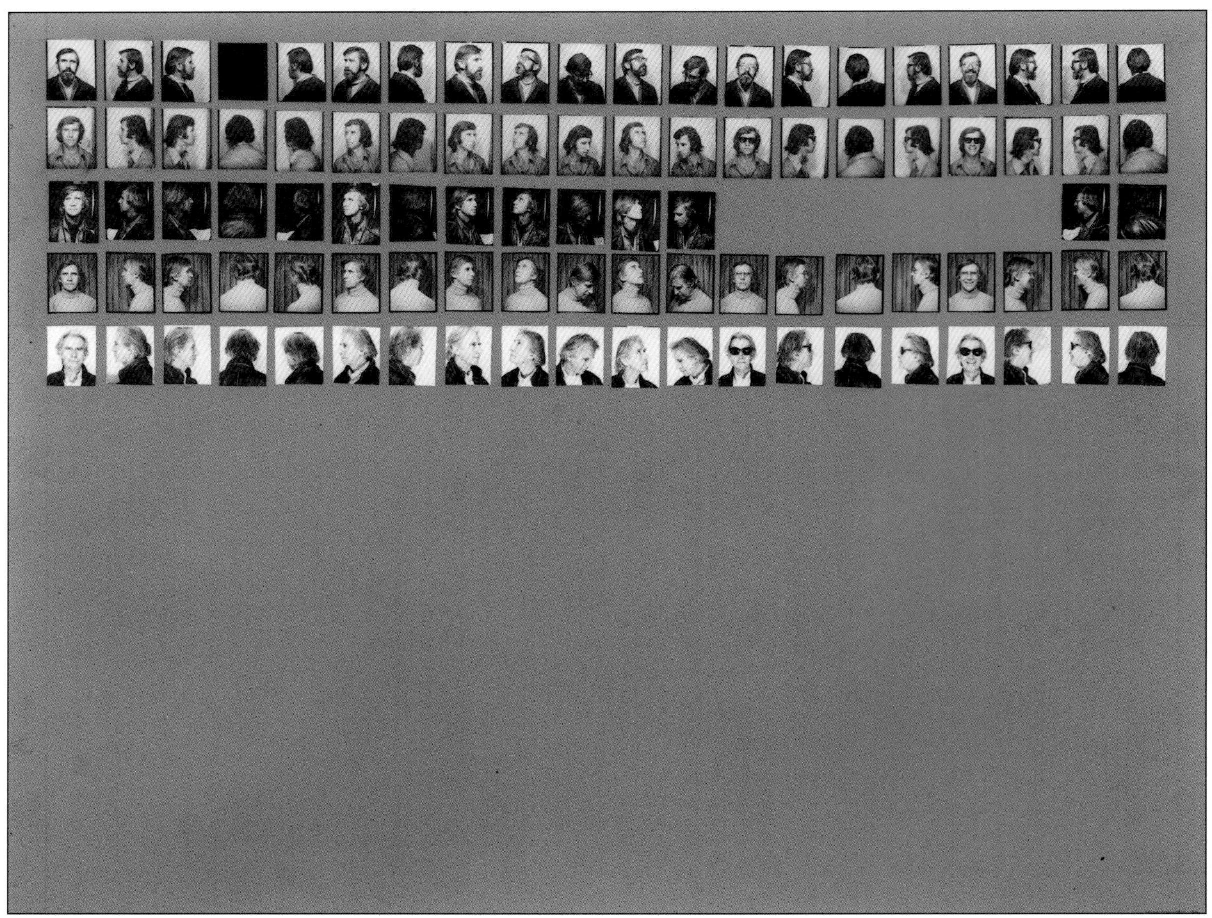

The Transfiguration, Discontinuity, and Degeneration of the Image, 1969-present
Arcade photographs mounted on board
Collection of the artist

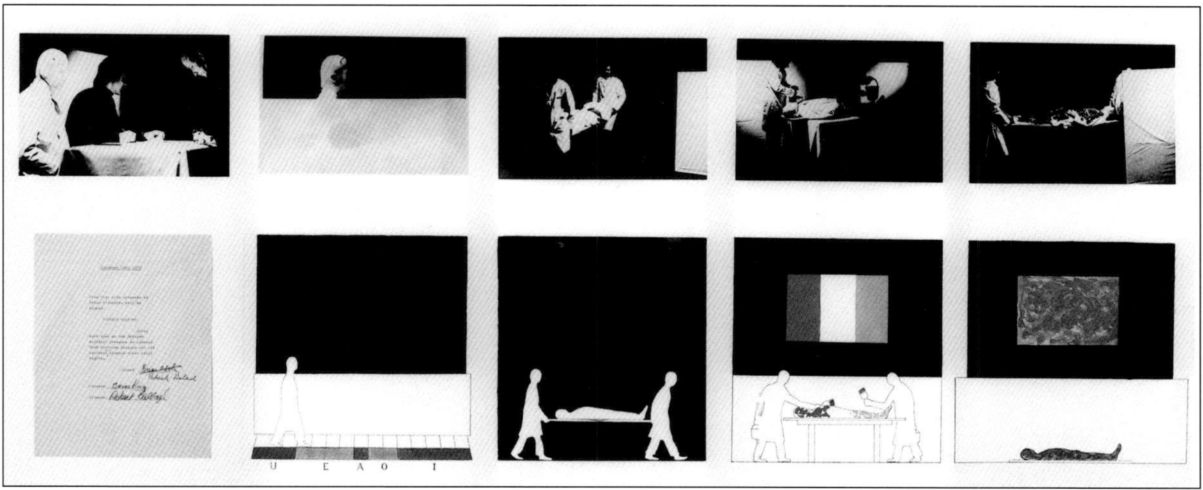

Name Change, 1972
Photographs, ink and gouache drawings on paper, typed text on paper collaged onto posterboard, $27\frac{7}{8}$ x 60 in.
Collection of the artist

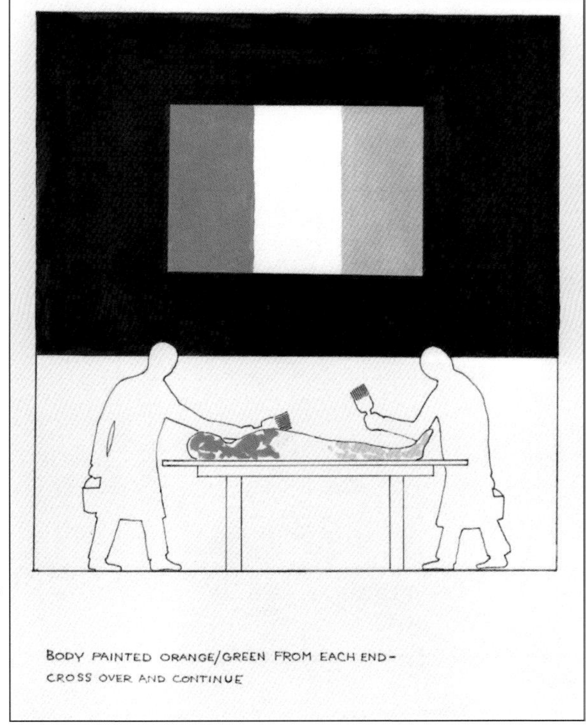

Name Change (Detail)

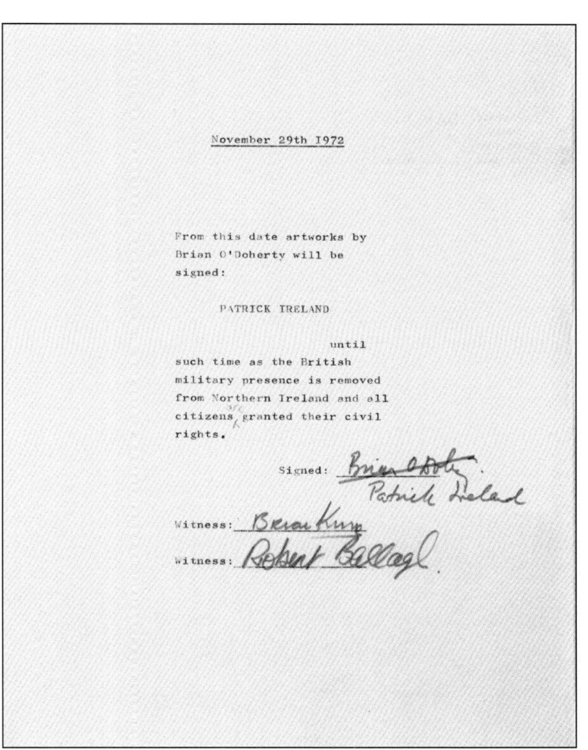

November 29th 1972

From this date artworks by
Brian O'Doherty will be
signed:

PATRICK IRELAND

until
such time as the British
military presence is removed
from Northern Ireland and all
citizens are granted their civil
rights.

Signed: Brian O'Doherty
Patrick Ireland

Witness: Brian King

Witness: Robert Ballagh

Name Change (Detail)

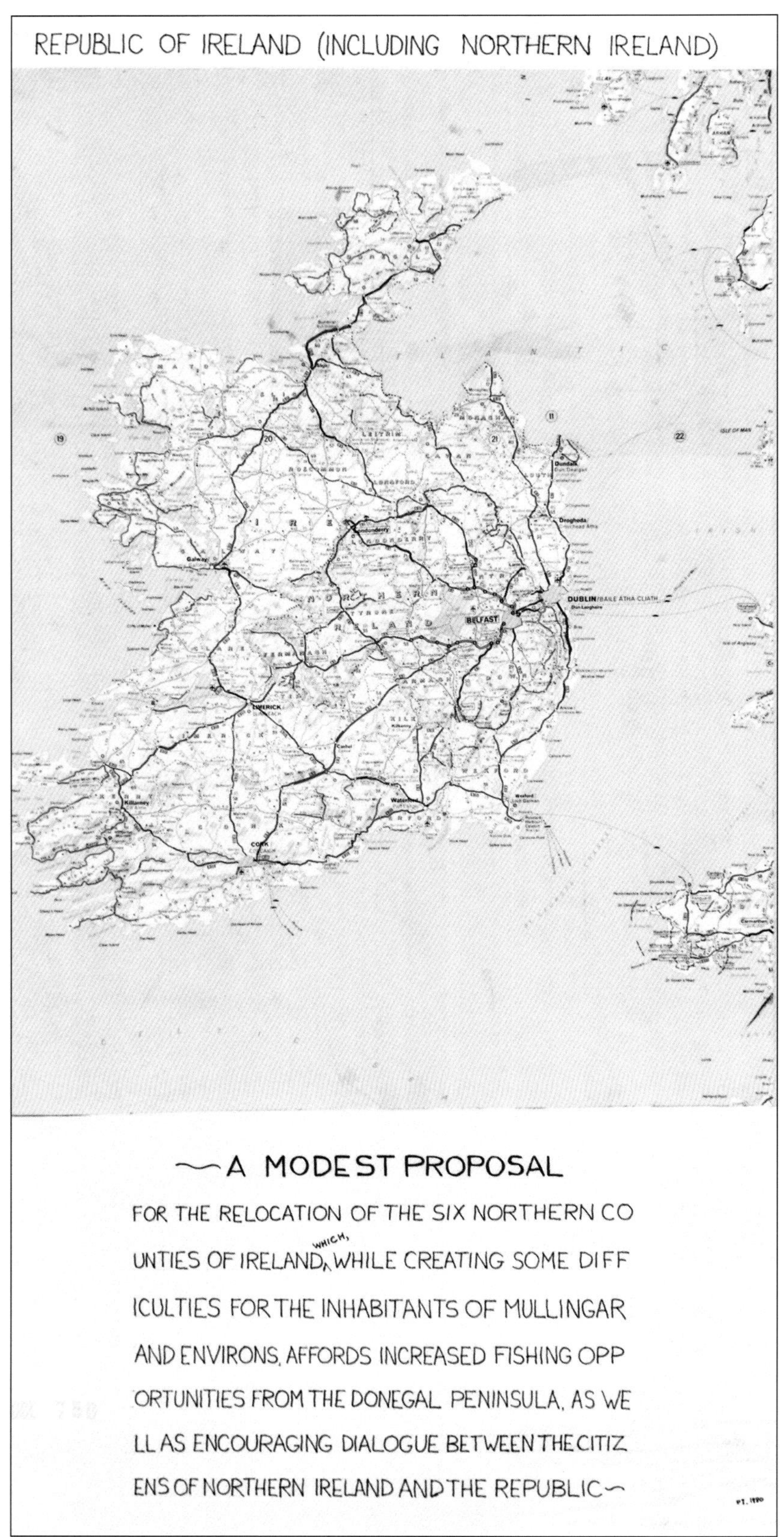

Ireland: A Modest Proposal, 1980
Collage on posterboard, 31½ x 16½ in.
Collection of the artist

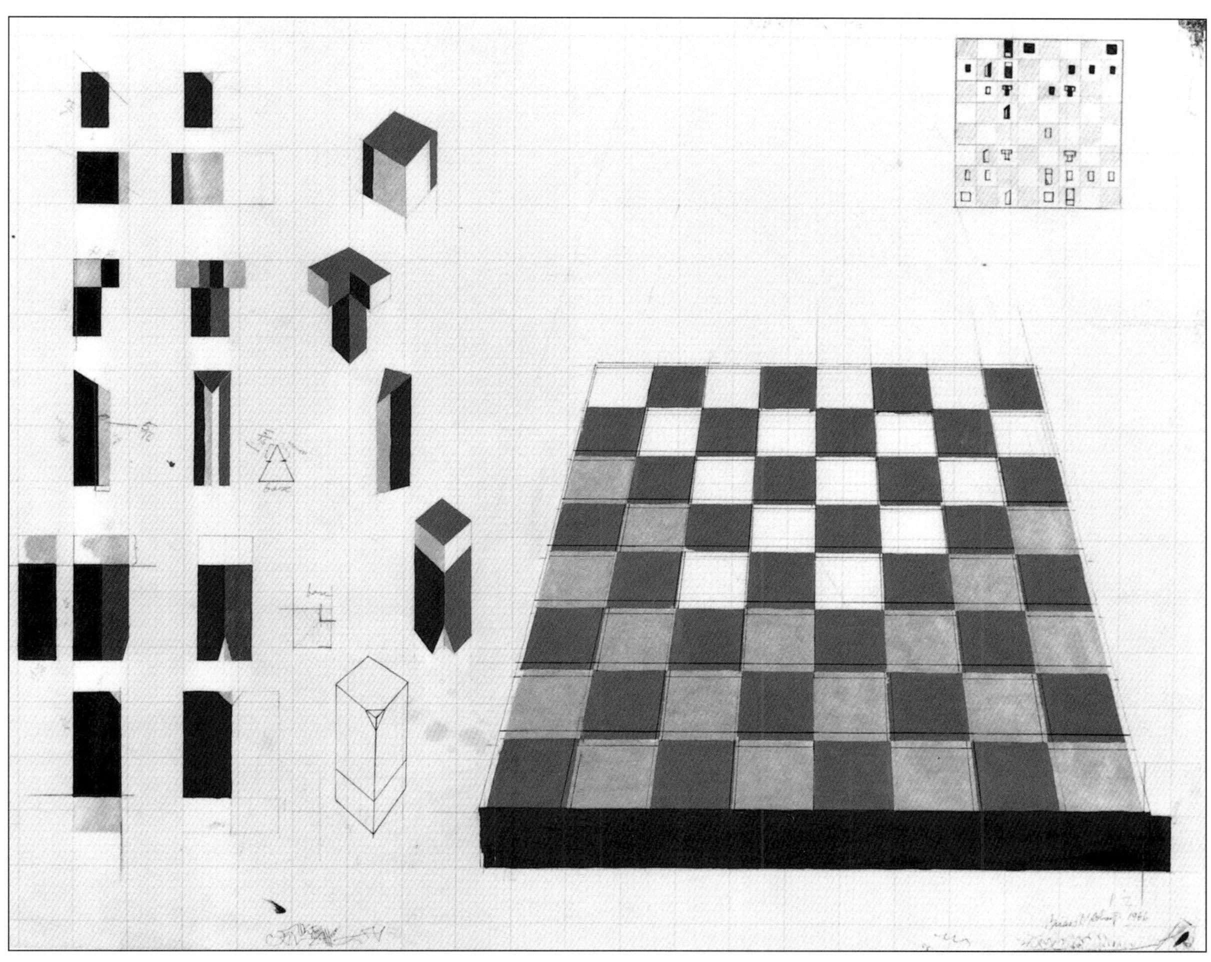

Chess set, 1966
Pen, gouache on graph paper, 17 x 22 in.
Collection of the artist

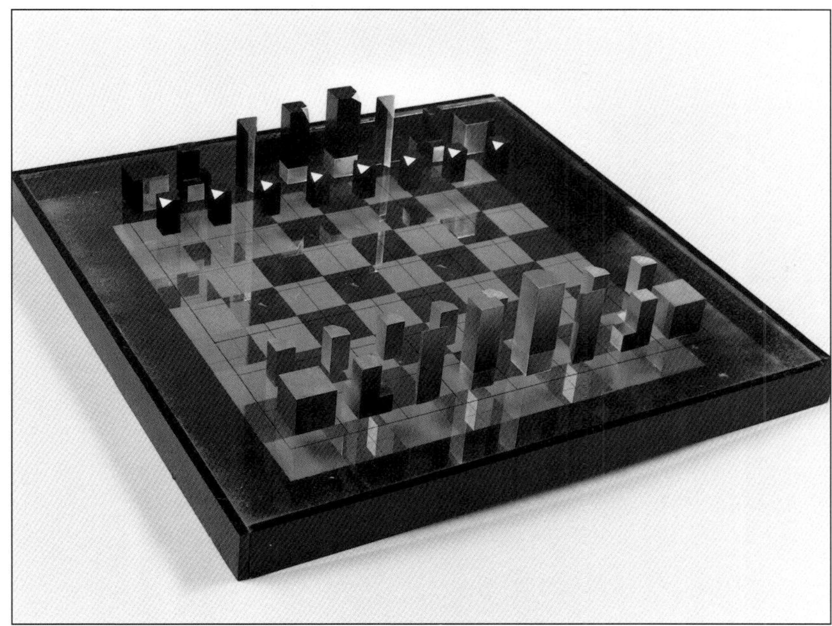

Chess Set, 1966
Metal, glass, gouache on mirror, board, 1 1/2 x 16 1/2 x 16 1/2 in.
Collection of the artist

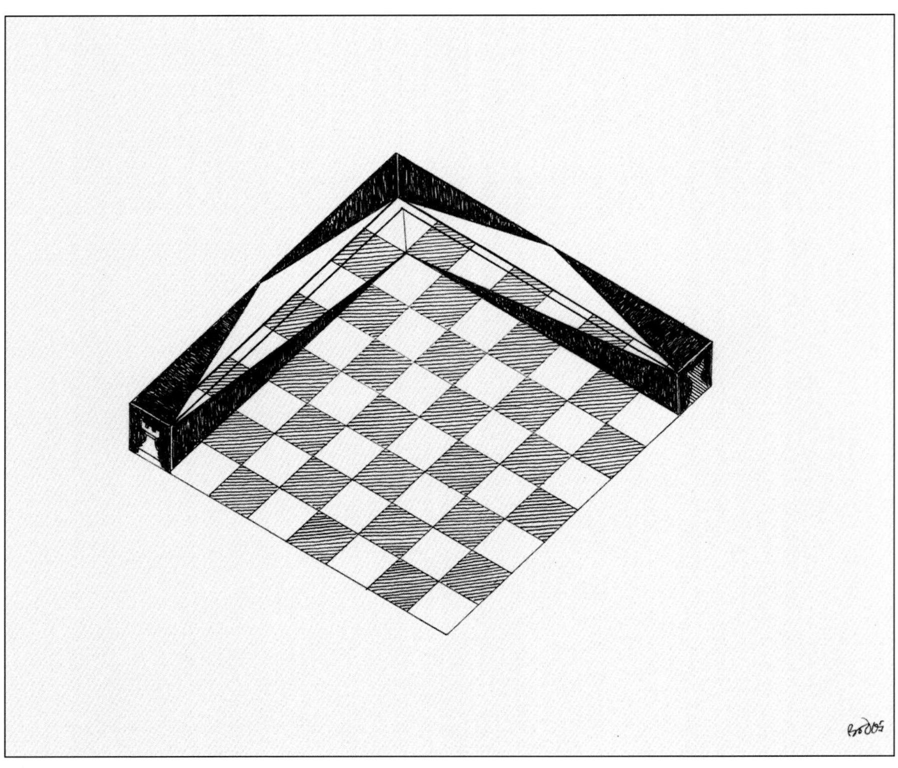

Castle Corner, 1965
Ink on paper, $8\frac{3}{4} \times 10\frac{3}{4}$ in.
Collection of the artist

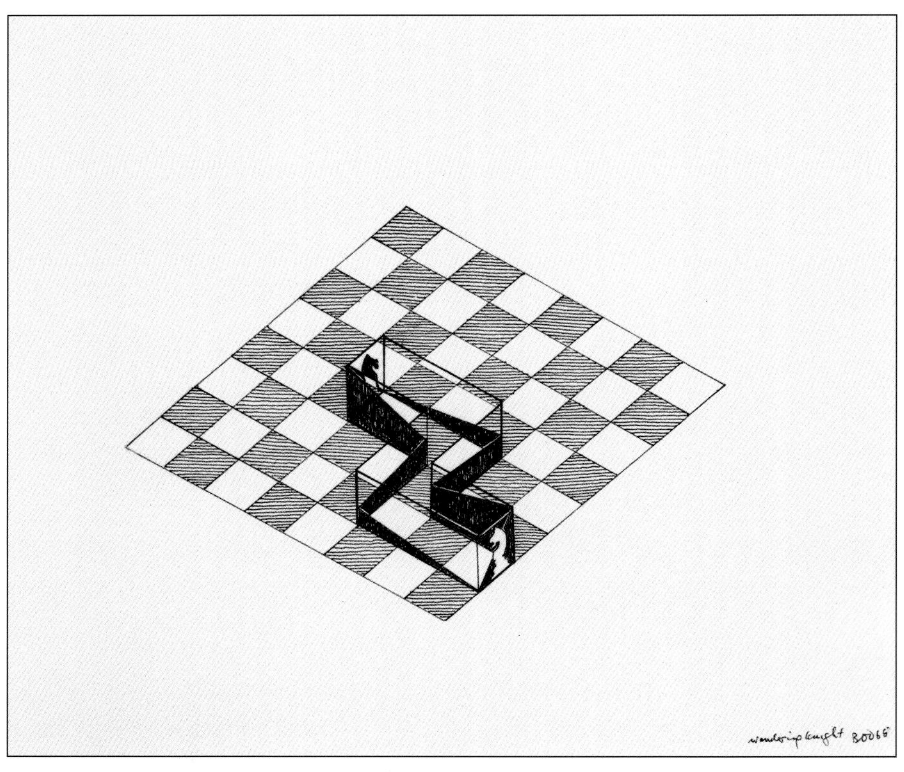

Wandering Knight, 1965
Ink on paper, $8\frac{3}{4} \times 10\frac{3}{4}$ in.
Collection of the artist

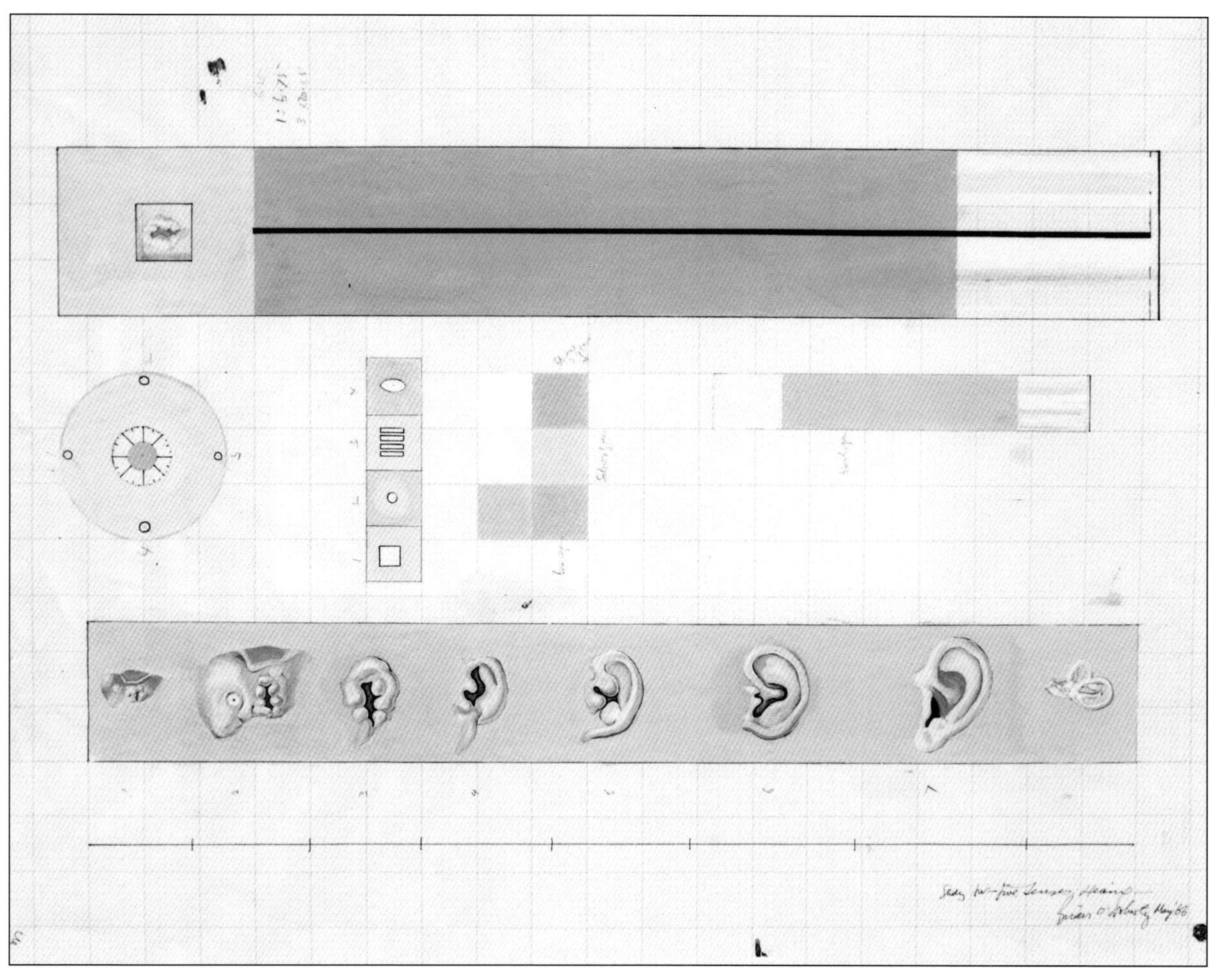

Study for the Five Senses: Hearing, 1966
Gouache, ink, and pencil on graph paper, 17 x 22 in.
Collection of the artist

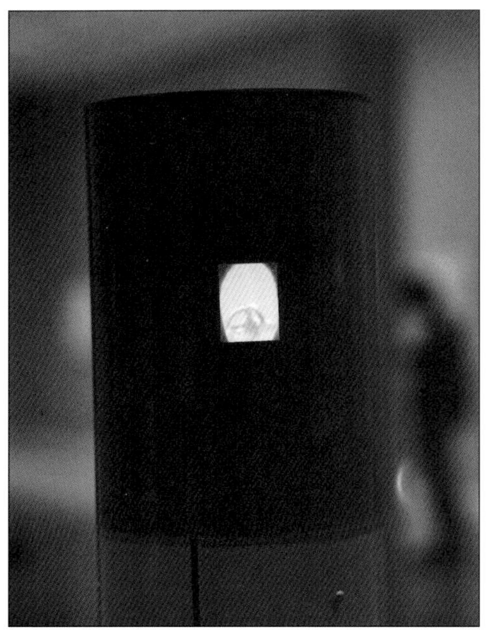

Hearing (Detail)

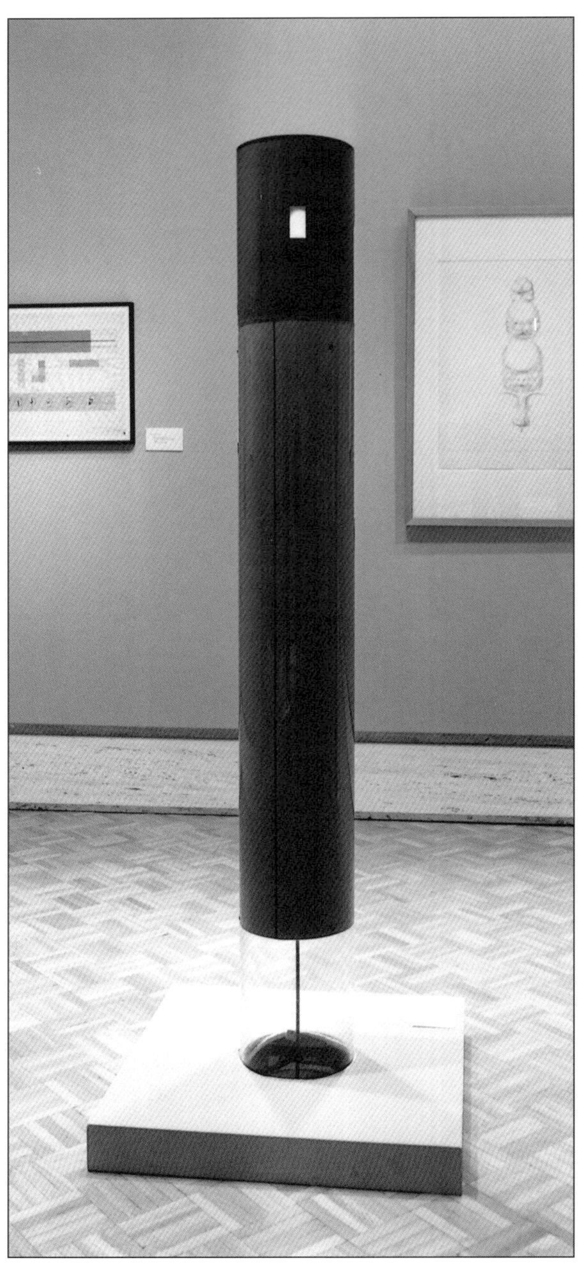

Hearing, 1966
Mixed media, H. 64 in., D. 8 in.
Collection of the artist

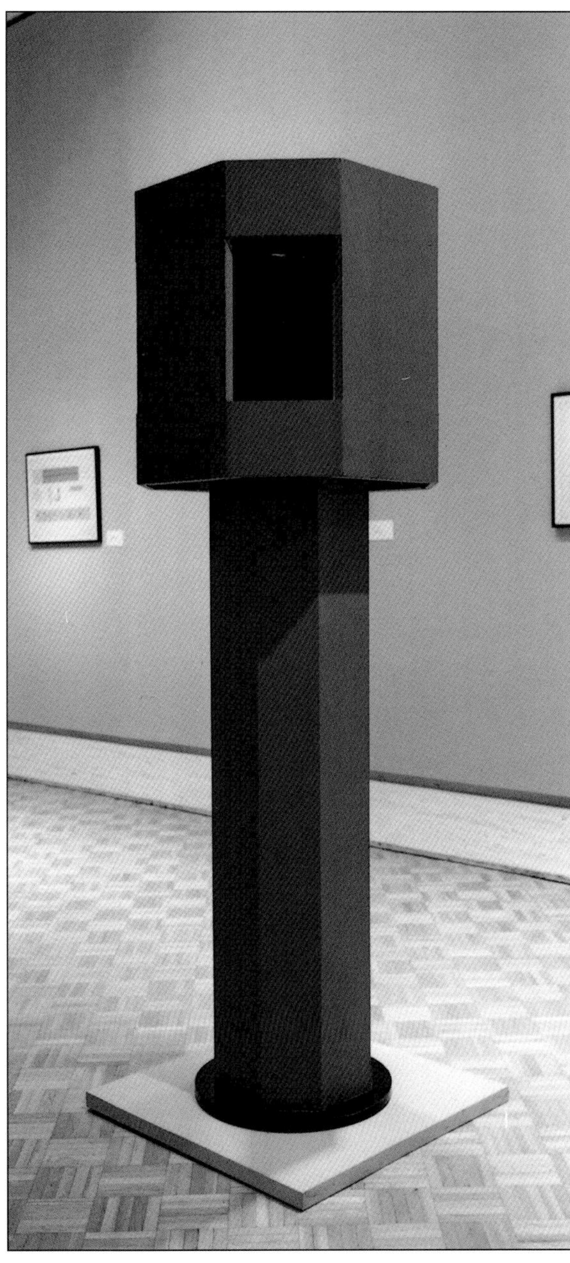

Sight (Narcissus), 1966
Mixed media, 73 x 23⅜ in.
Collection of the artist

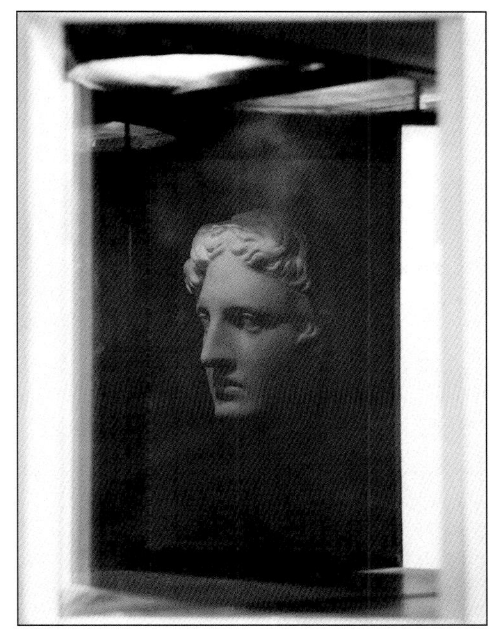

Sight (Narcissus) (Detail)

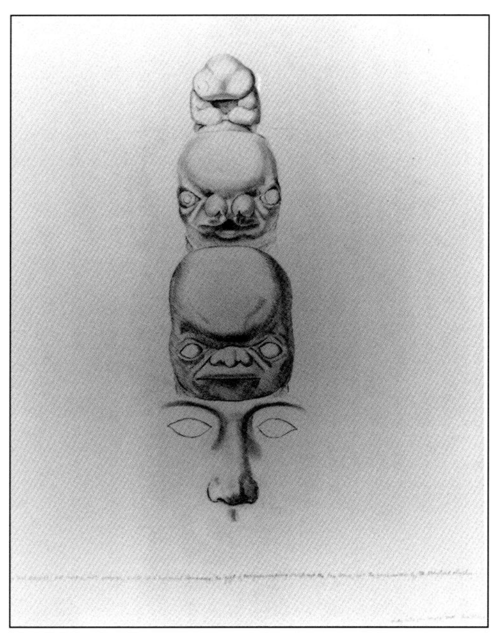

Smell, 1966–67
Pencil on paper, 26¾ x 23 in.
Collection of the artist

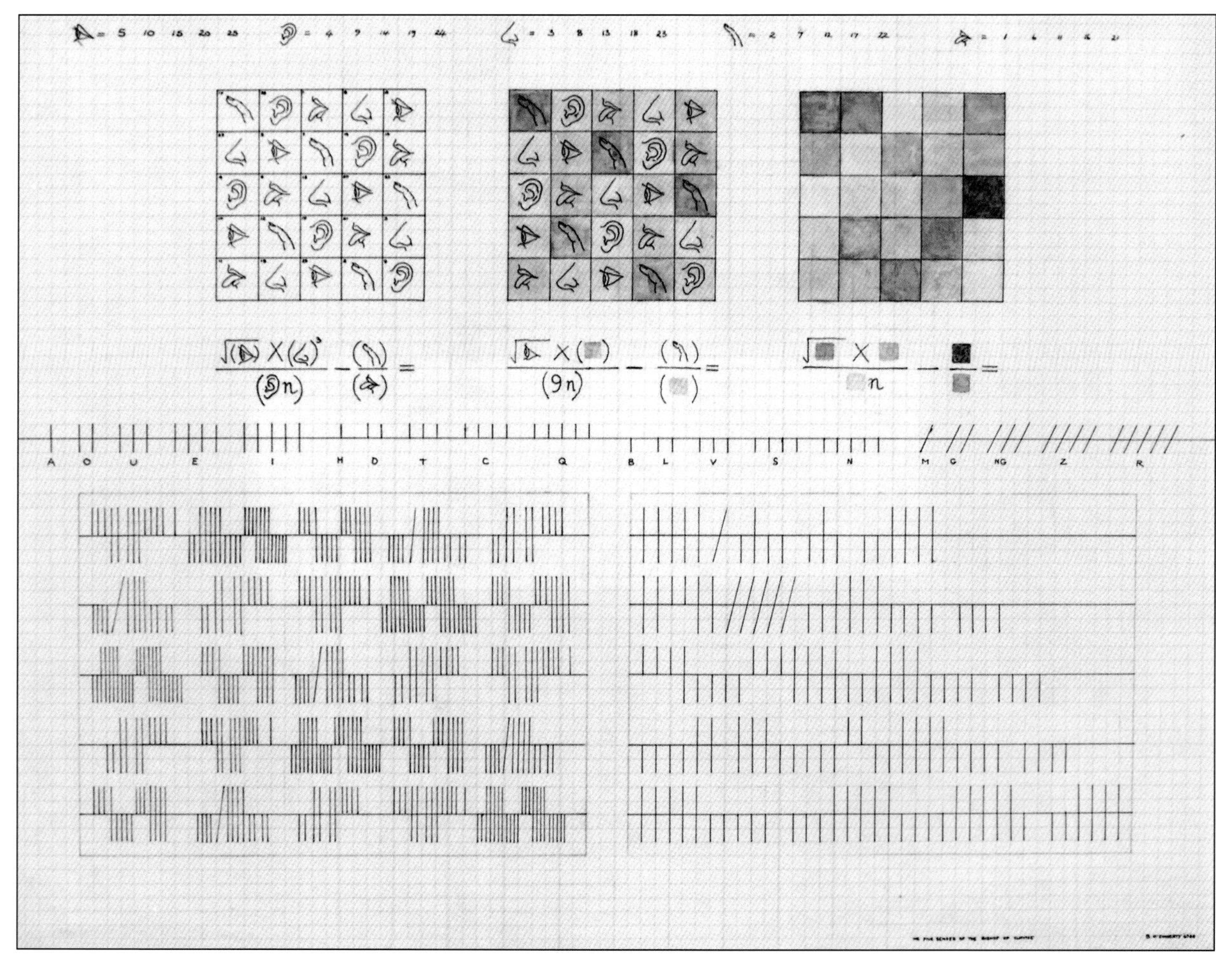

The Five Senses of the Bishop of Cloyne, 1967–68
Ink and watercolor on graph paper, 17 x 22 in.
Collection of the artist

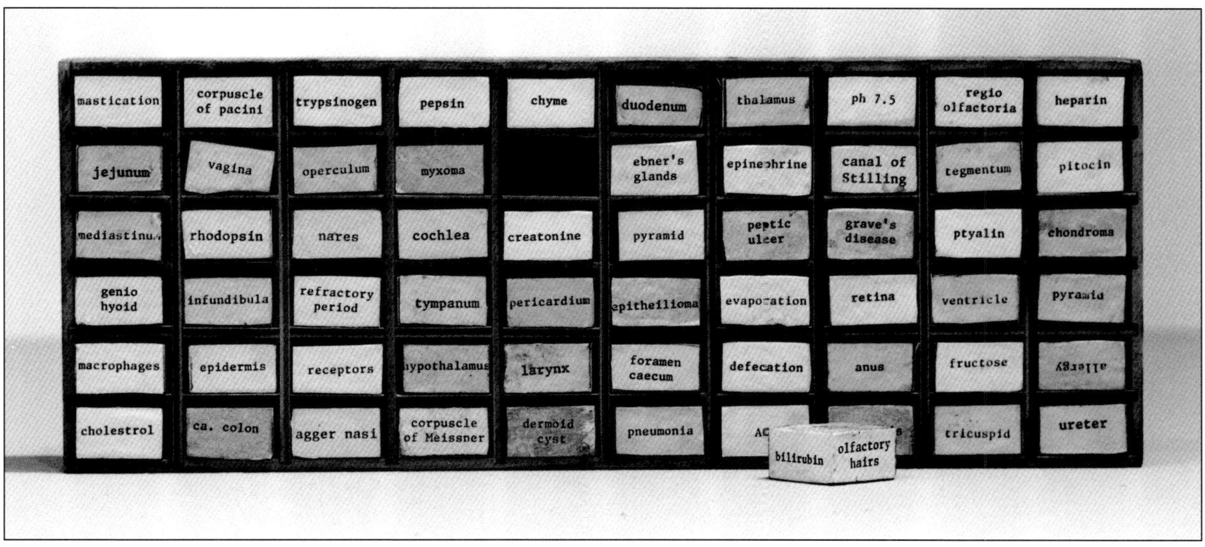

Kips Bay: The Body and Its Discontents, 1964
Mixed media, 4⅛ x 11 x 1½ in.
Collection of the artist

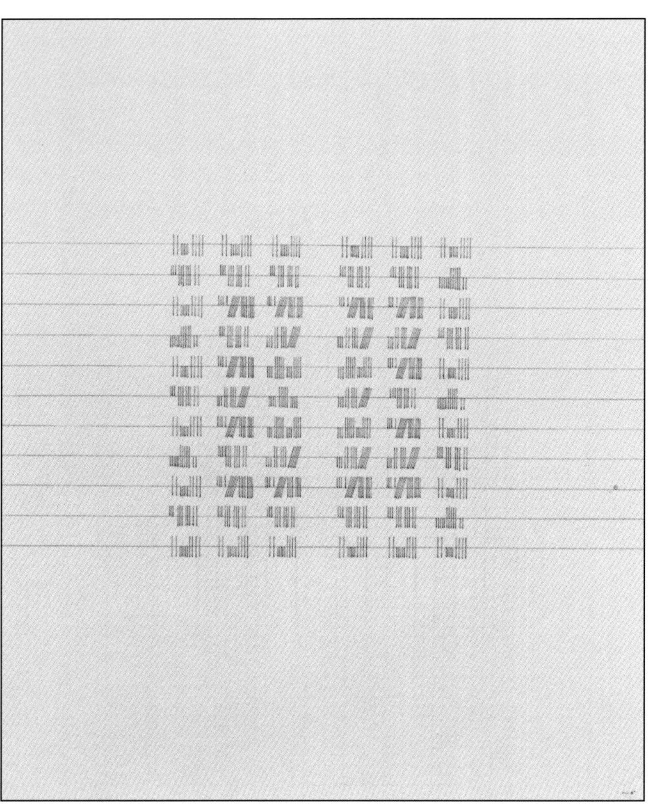

One to Five, 1967
Ink on graph paper, 22 x 17 in.
Collection of the artist

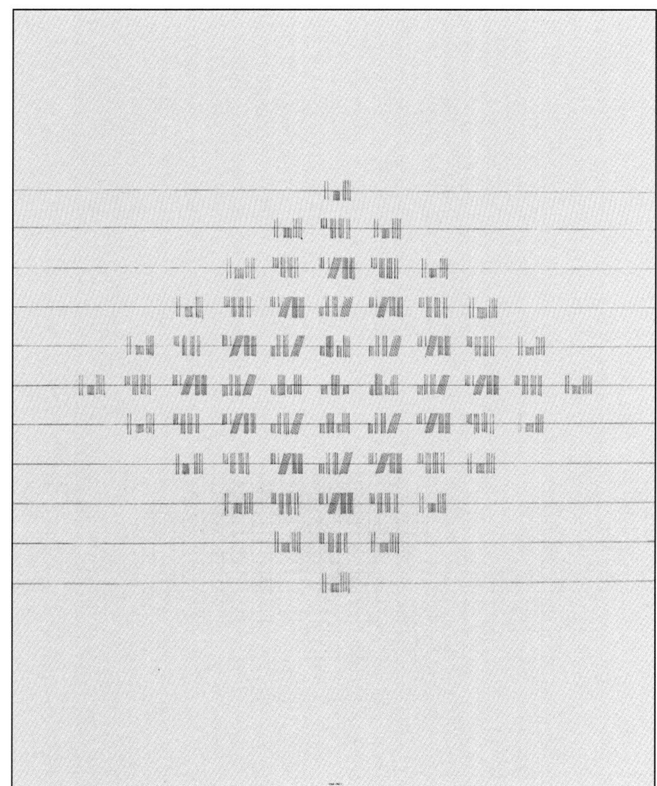

One to Five Rotated, 1967
Ink on paper on graph paper, 22 x 17 in.
Collection of the artist

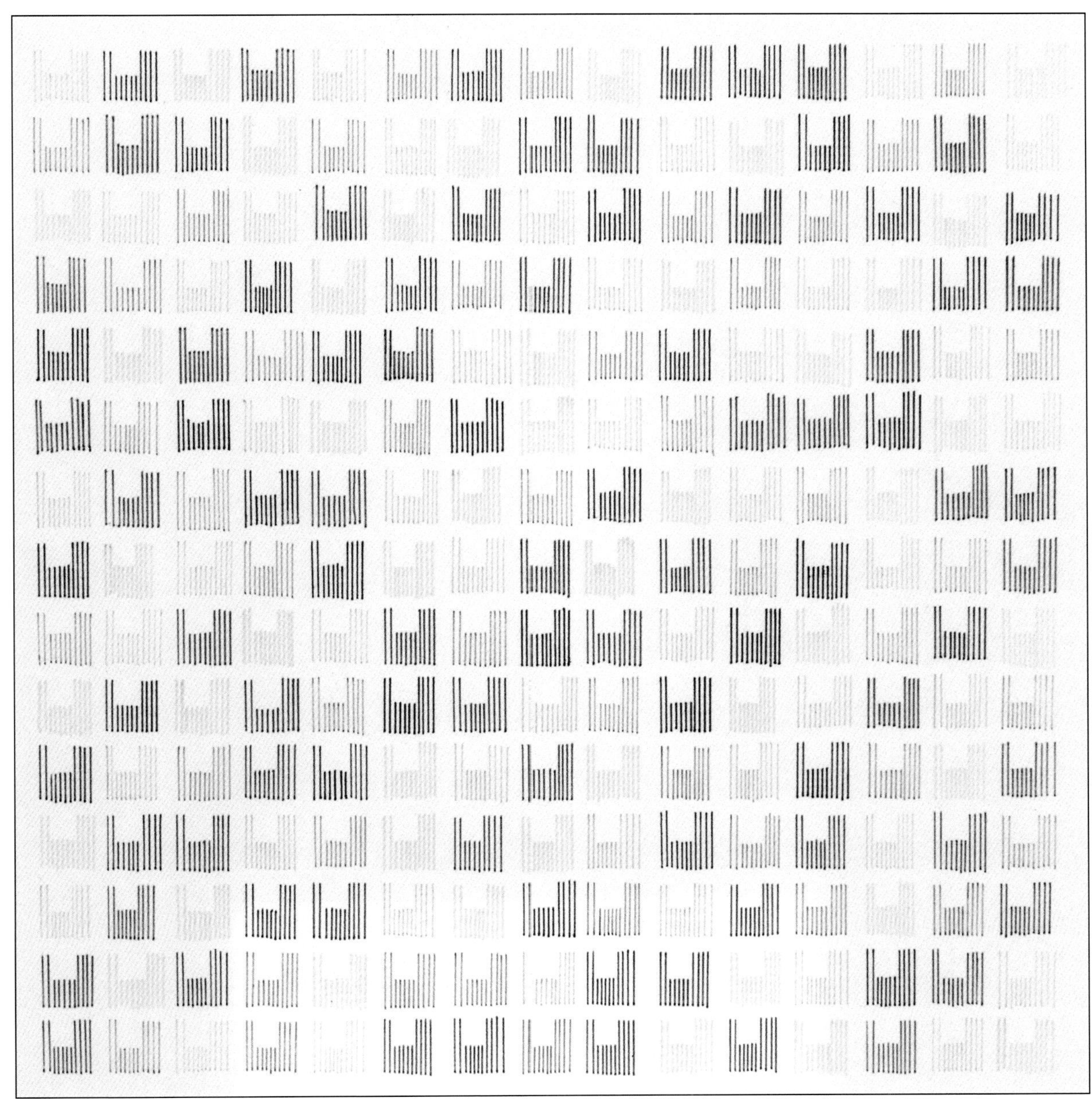

One Drawing, 1969
Colored inks on paper, 23 x 29 in.
Collection of the artist

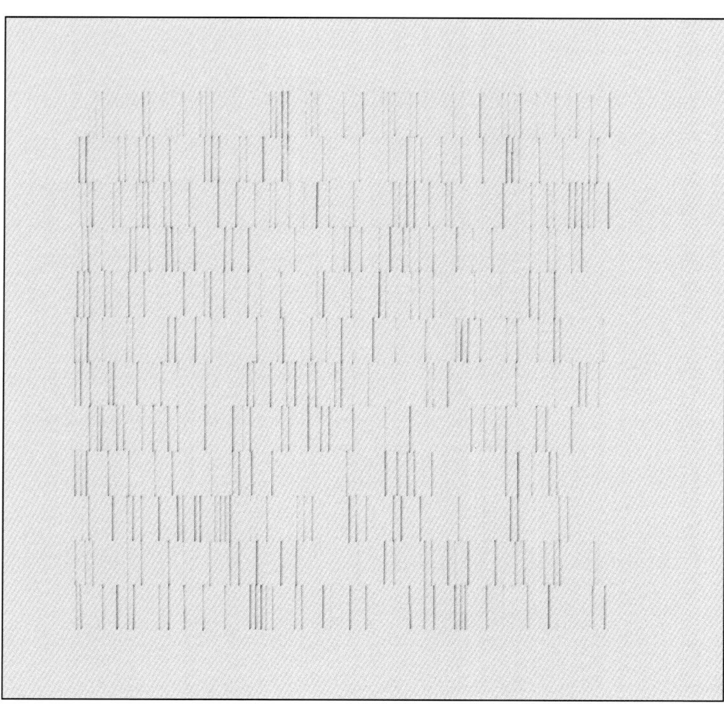

Single Vowel Drawing, 1970
Colored inks on paper, 23 x 29 in.
Collection of the artist

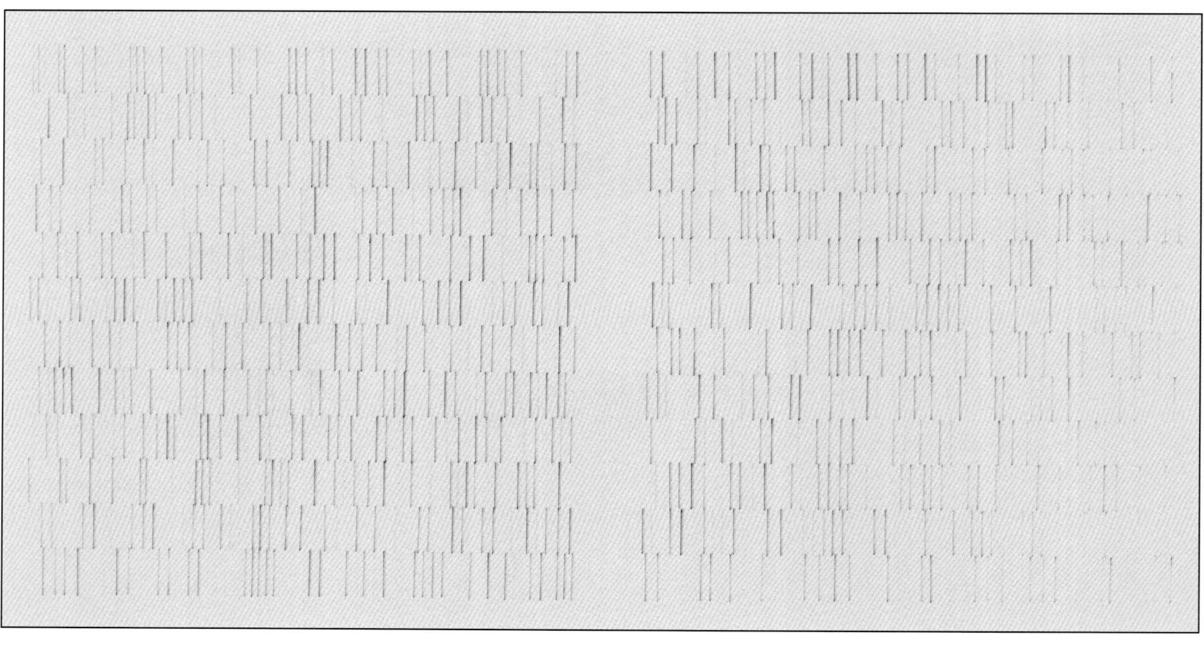

Double Vowel Drawing, 1971
Colored inks on paper, 23 x 29 in.
Collection of the artist

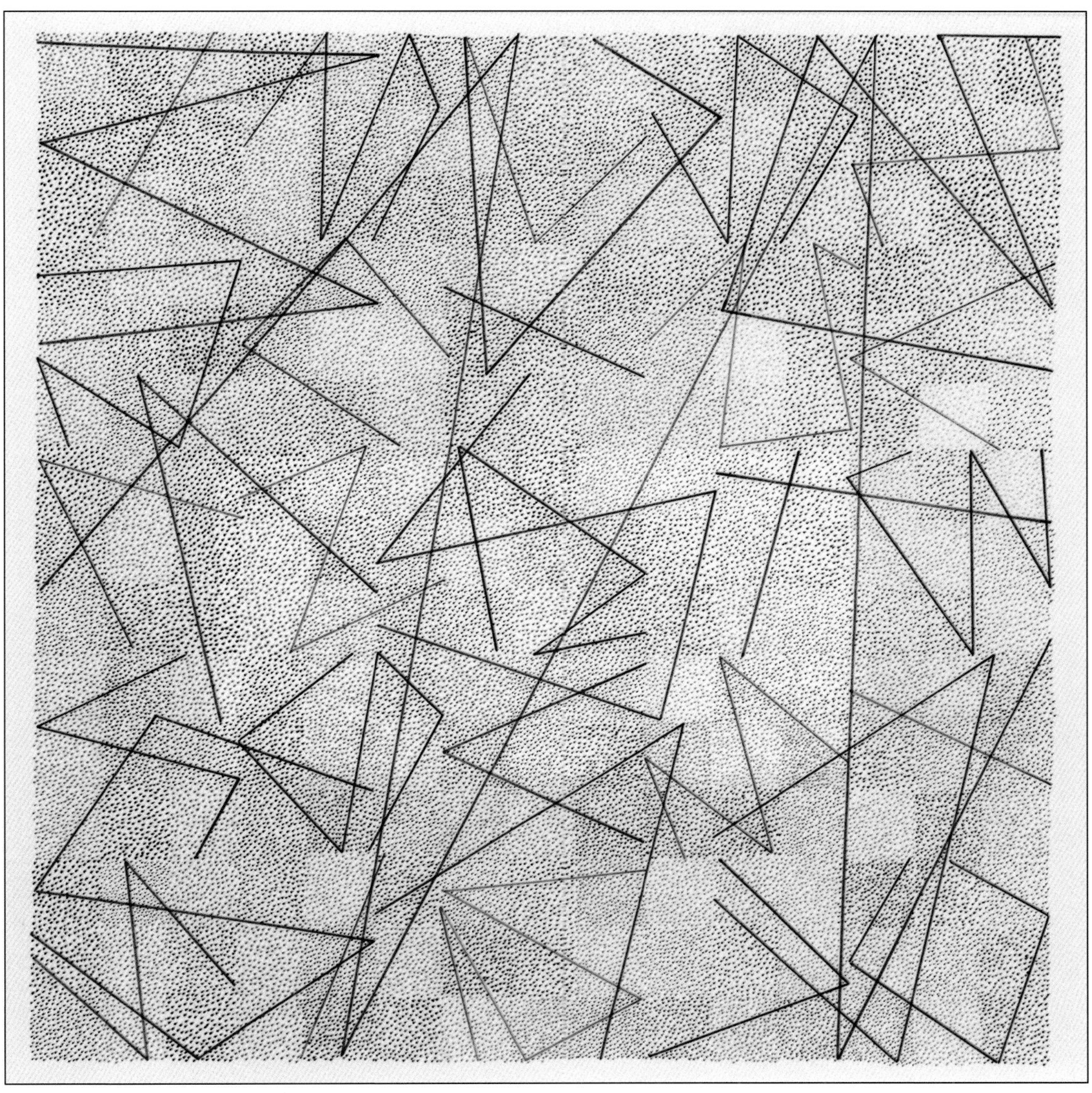

Angled Vowels at Three Scales, 1975
Colored inks on paper, 23 x 29 in.
Collection of the artist

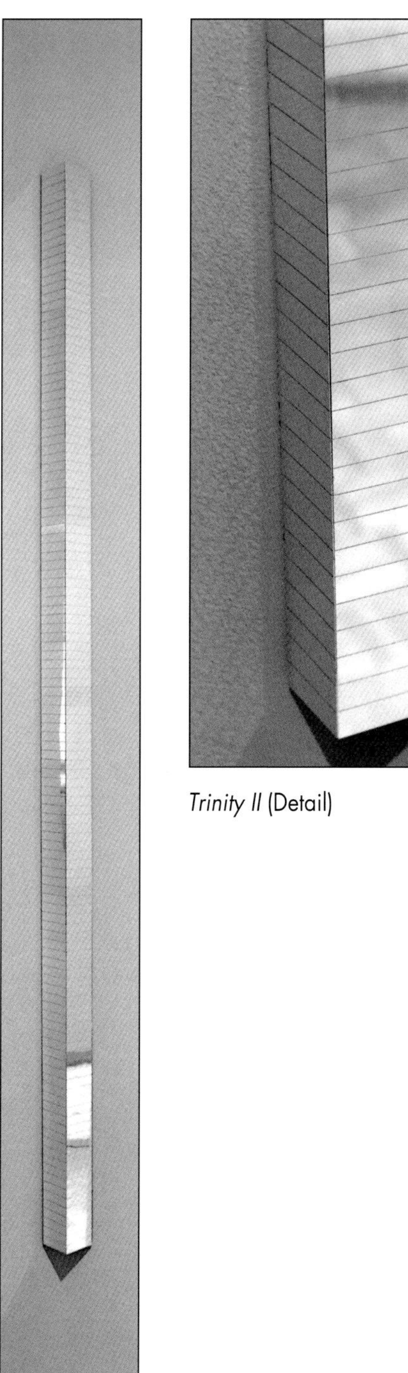

Trinity II (Detail)

Trinity II, 1967
Polished aluminum on wood, 60 x 2¾ x 1½ in.
Collection of the artist

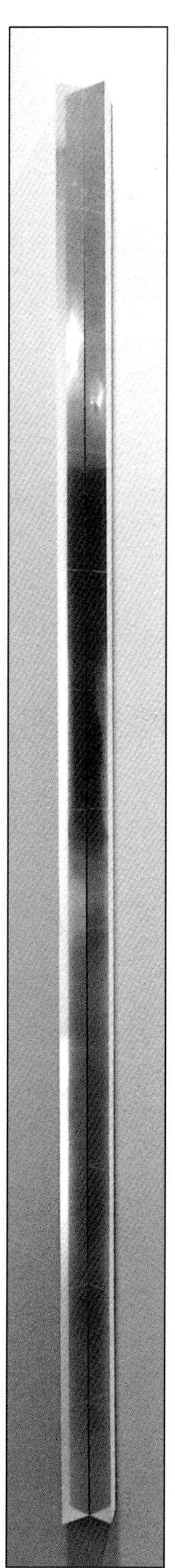

One, 1969
Polished aluminum on wood, 84 x 2⅞ x 2⅝ in.
Collection of the artist

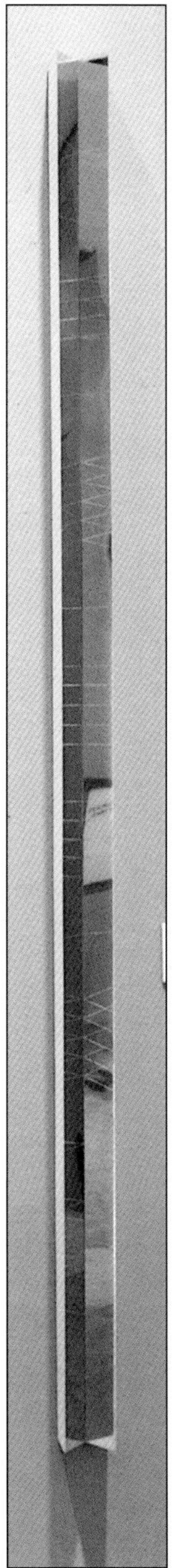

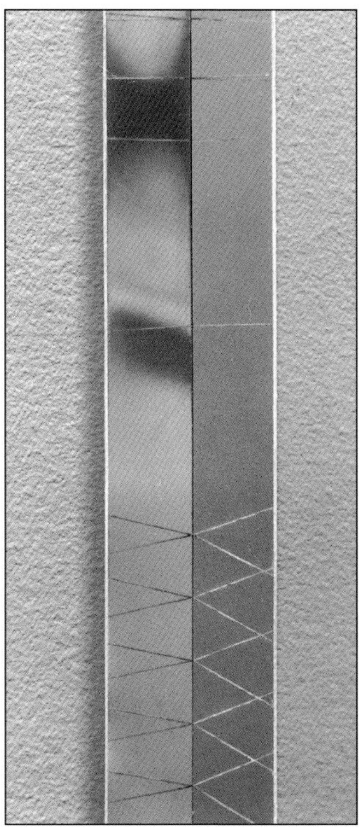

Meribah (Detail)

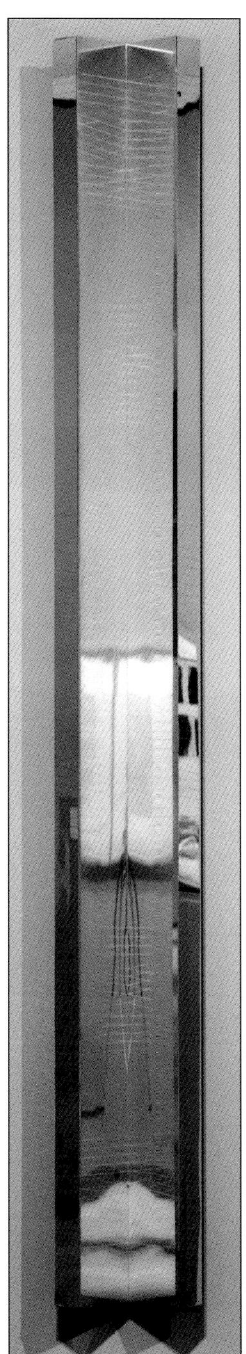

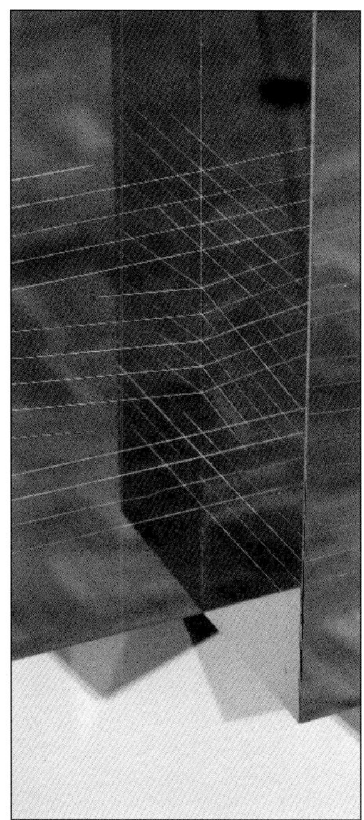

Annso (Here) (Detail)

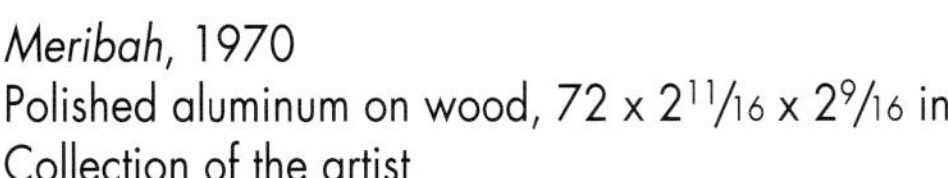

Meribah, 1970
Polished aluminum on wood, 72 x $2\frac{11}{16}$ x $2\frac{9}{16}$ in.
Collection of the artist

Annso (Here), 1970
Polished aluminum on wood, 72 x $8\frac{1}{2}$ x $4\frac{1}{4}$ in.
Elvehjem Museum of Art Endowment Fund, Juli Plant Grainger Endowment Fund, Cyril W. Nave Endowment Fund purchase, 1992.335

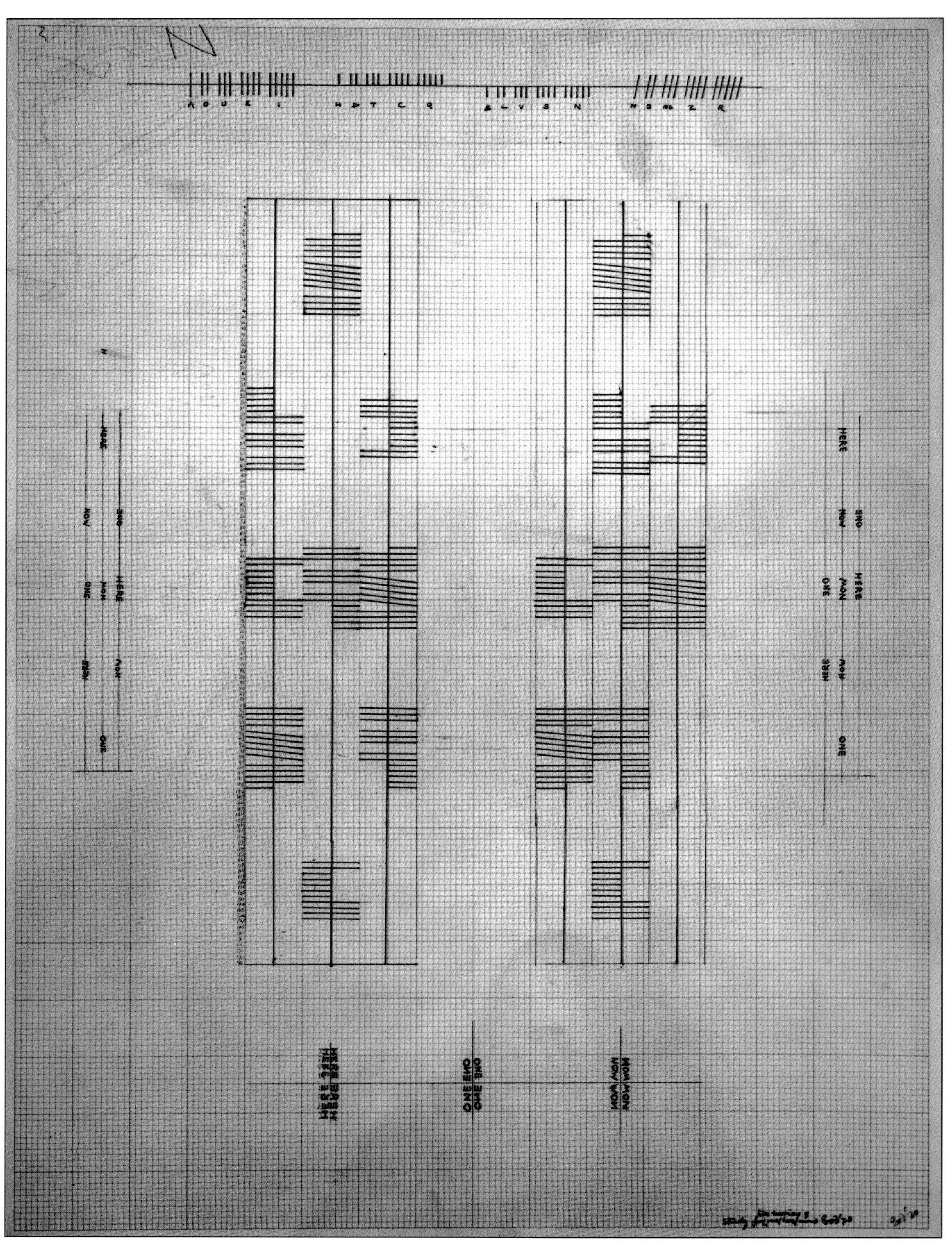

Study for Two Versions of One/Here/Now, 1970
Ink on graph paper, 22 x 17 in.
Collection of the artist

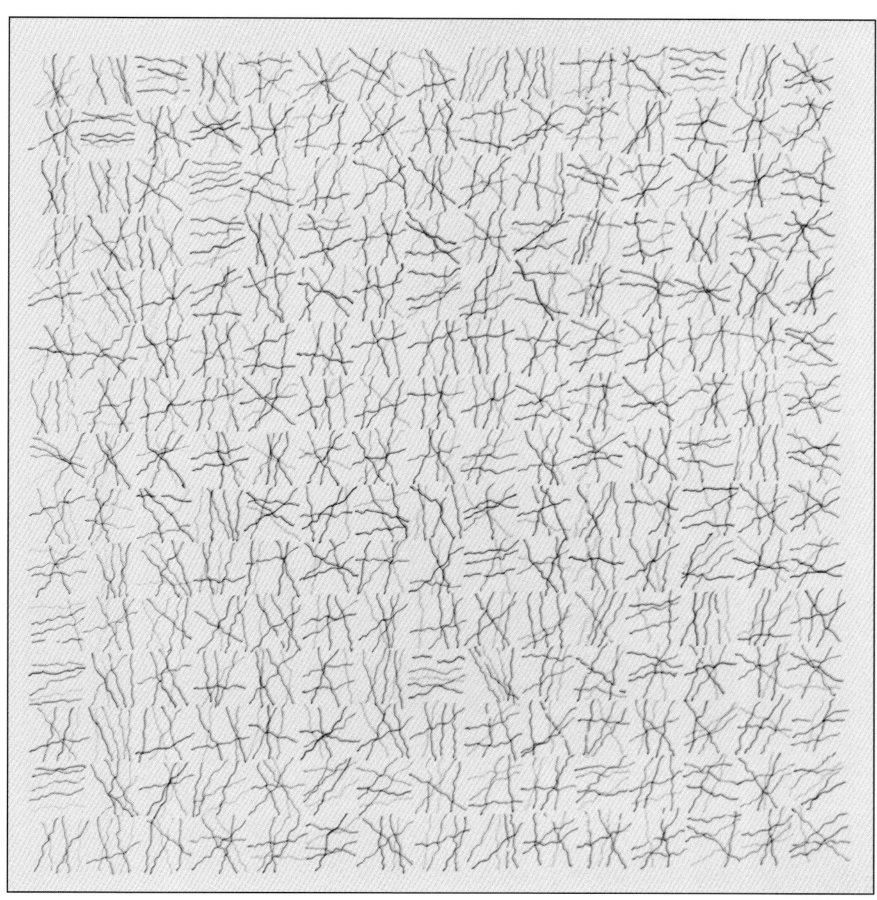

225 I's, Overlapping Crooked Lines, 1971
Colored inks on paper, 23 x 29 in.
Collection of the artist

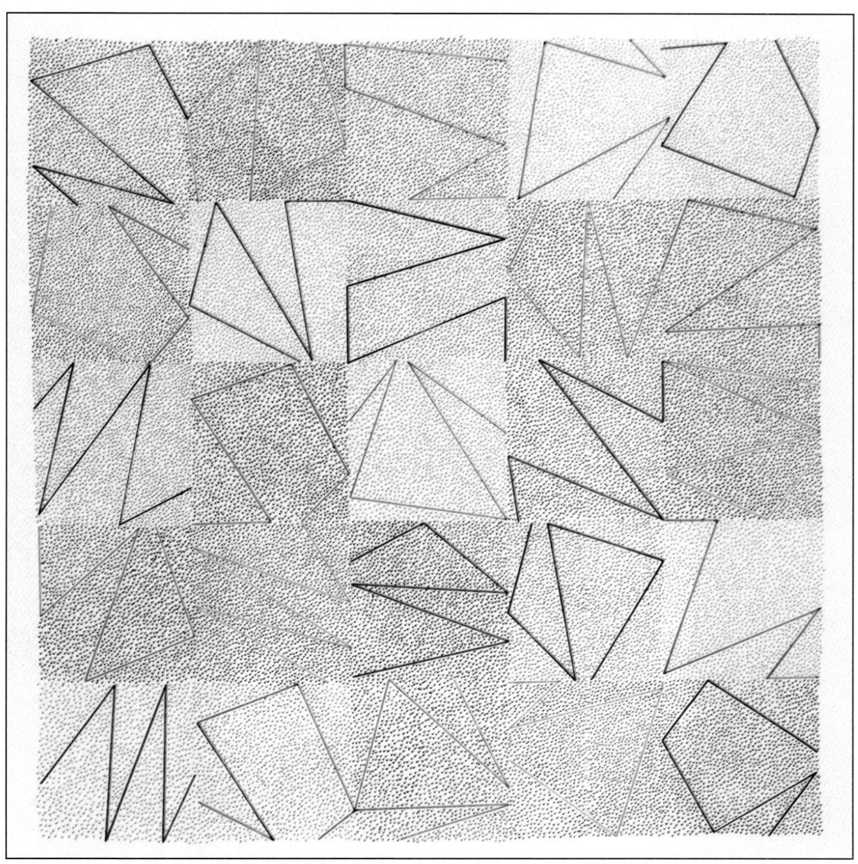

Twenty-five Angled I's on a Five-color 5 x 5 Point Grid, 1975
Colored inks on paper, 23 x 29 in.
Collection of the artist

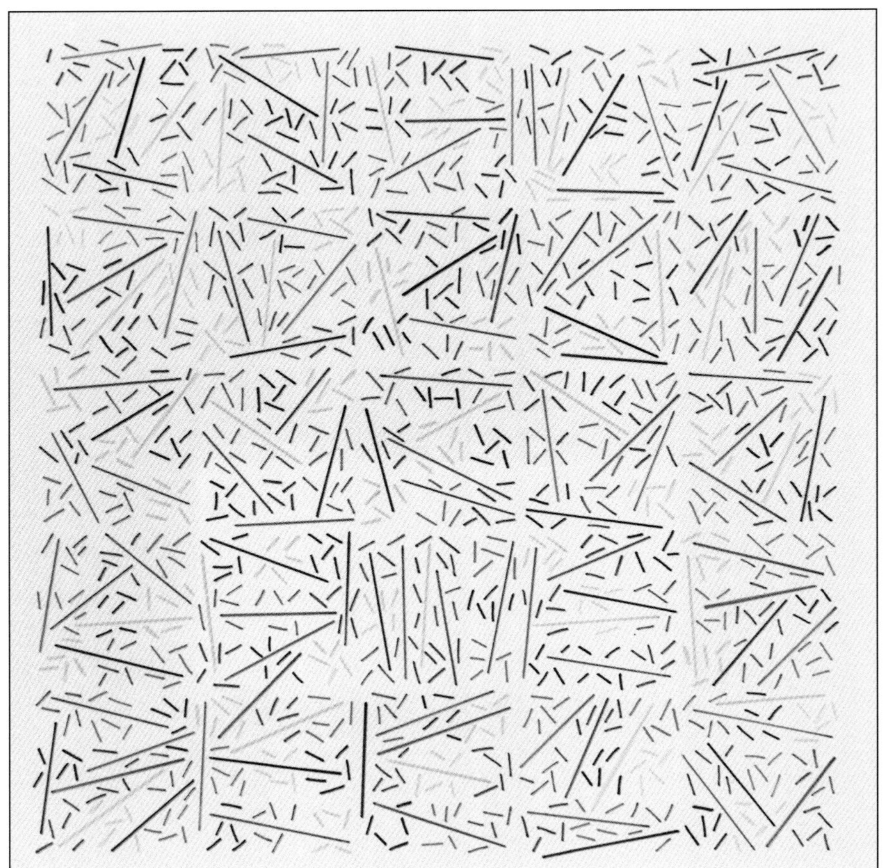

Five's with Broken Lines at Two Scales, 1975
Colored inks on paper, 23 x 29 in.
Collection of the artist

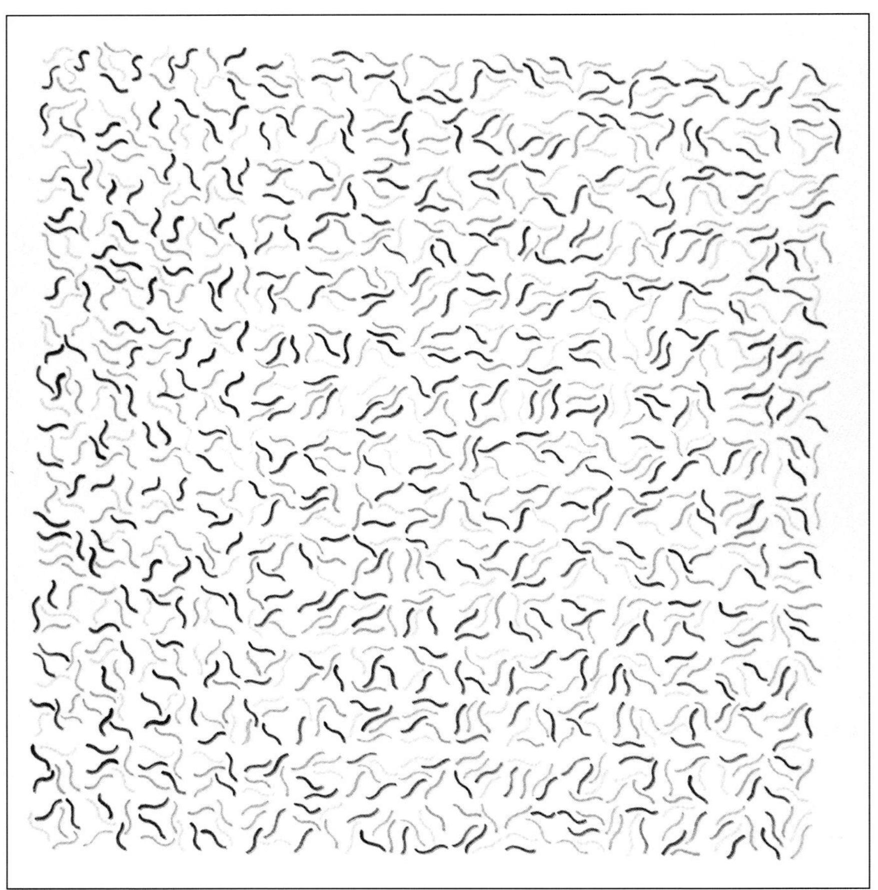

Snake I's, 1977
Colored inks on paper, 23 x 29 in.
Collection of the artist

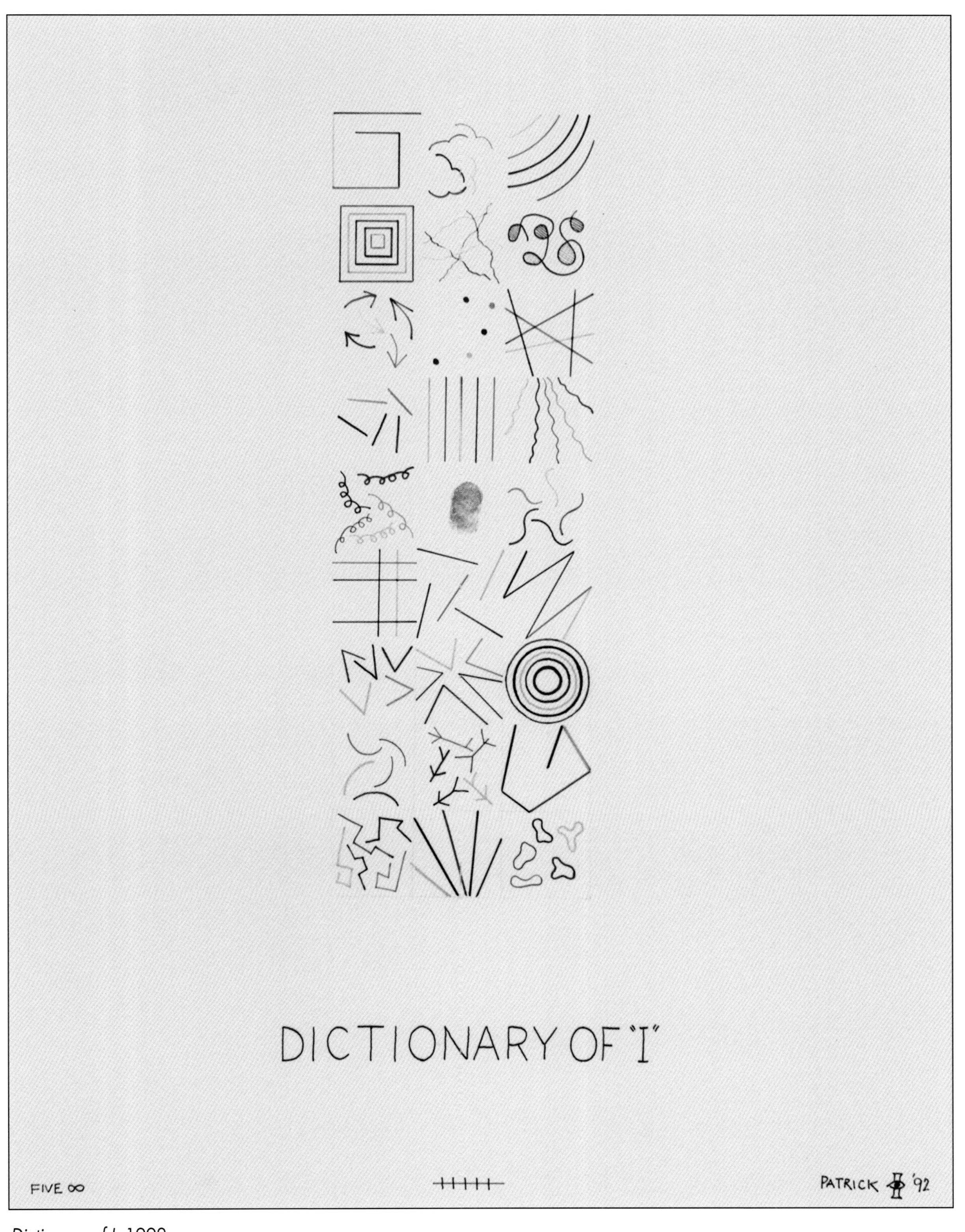

Dictionary of I, 1992
Pencil and colored inks on paper, 30 x 22½ in.
Collection of the artist

For Malevitch Even Though . . ., 1977
Colored ink on paper, 23 x 28 7/8 in.
Collection of Renato Danese

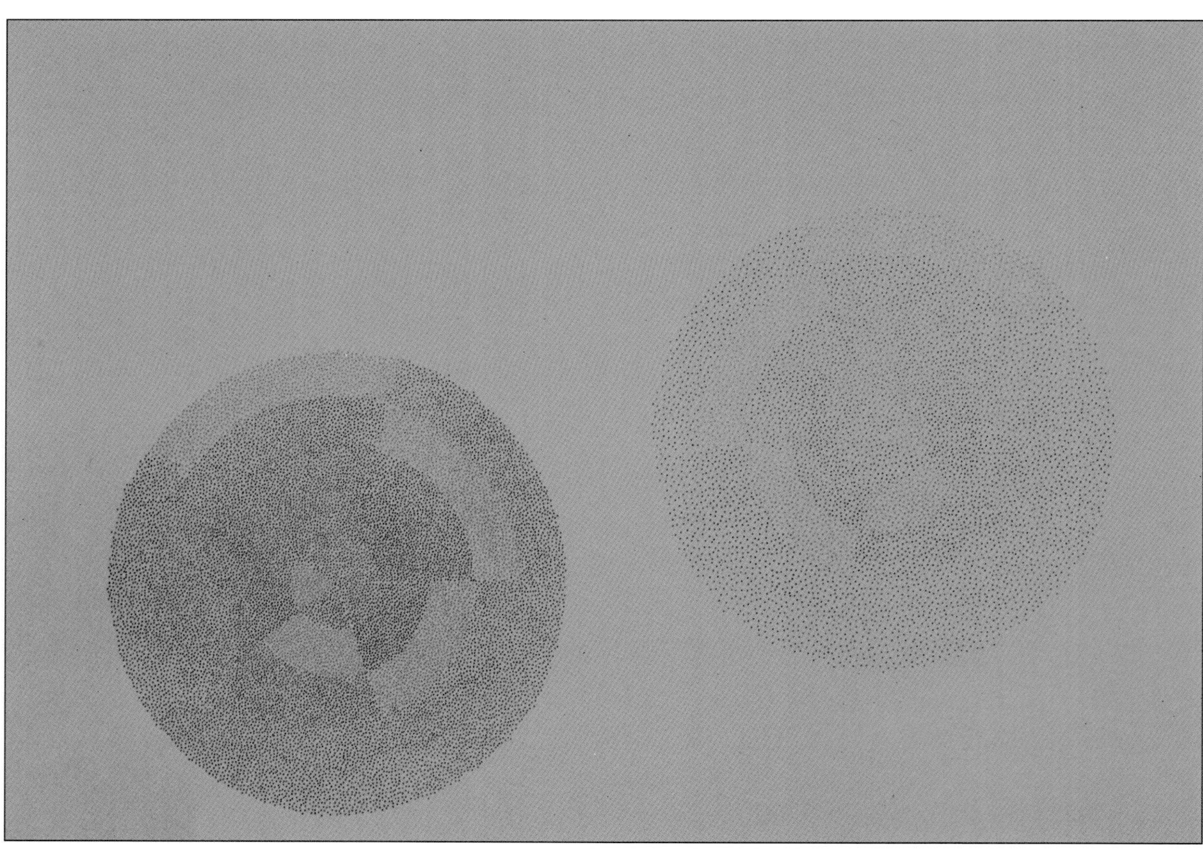

Rotating Circle with Echo, 1976
Colored inks and pencil on paper, 23 x 29 in.
Collection of the artist

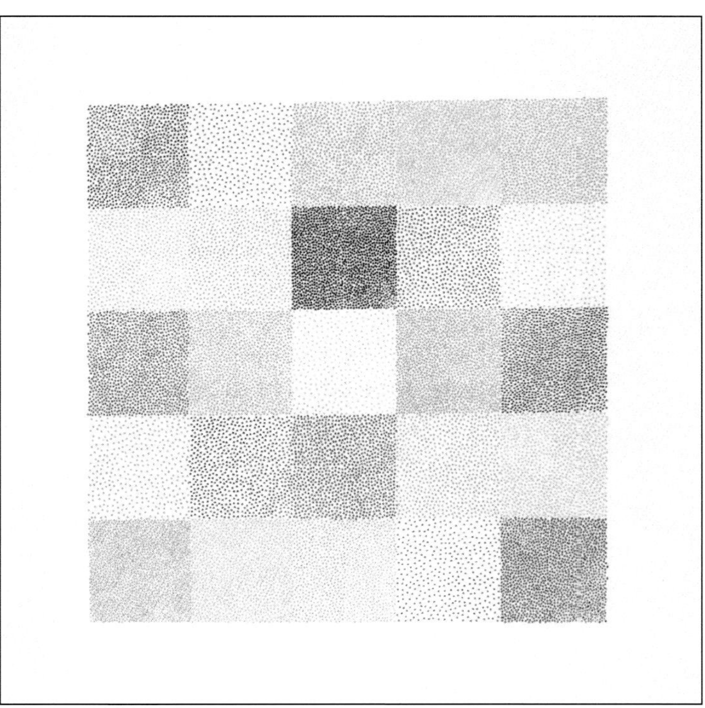

Five by Five, (Aerial Perspective) Five colors progressively at 1500, 1225, 950, 650, and 400 Points, 1977
Colored inks on paper, 23 x 29 in.
Collection of Barbara Novak

Ziggurat and Reflection, 1979
Colored inks on paper, 29 x 23 1/8 in.
Collection of the artist

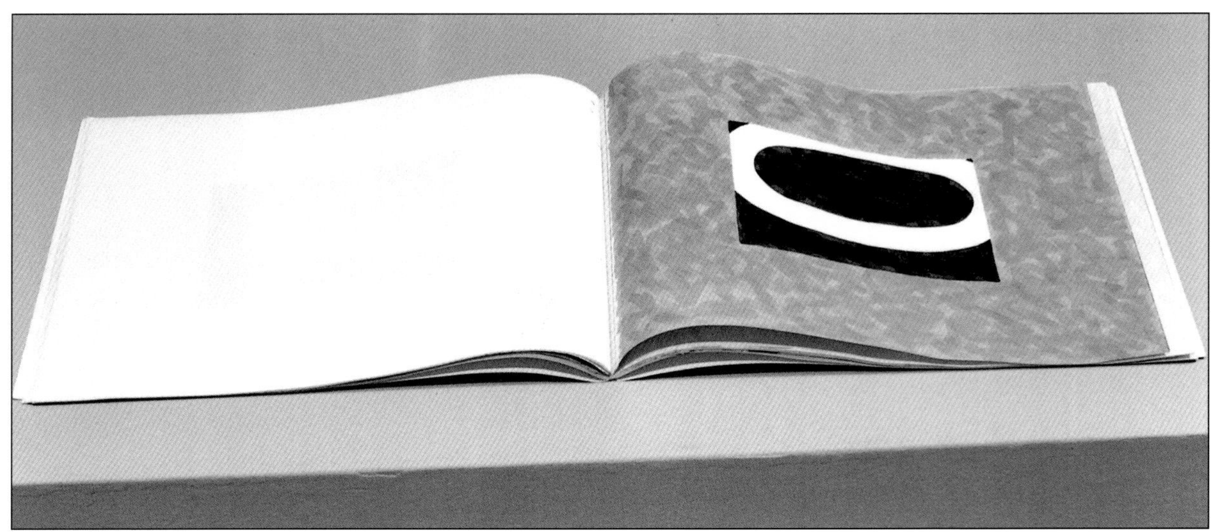

Barbara's Alphabet, 1979–80
Watercolor on paper, 8¼ x 11 in.
Collection of Barbara Novak

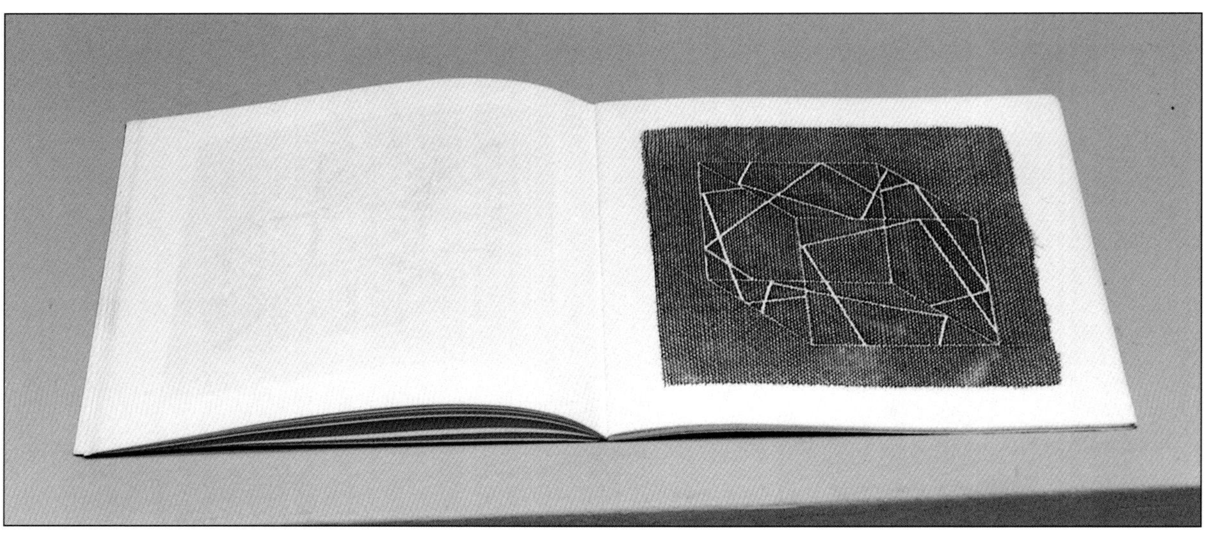

Inside the White Cube, ca. 1975
Colored inks on paper, 8 x 8 in.
Collection of Barbara Novak

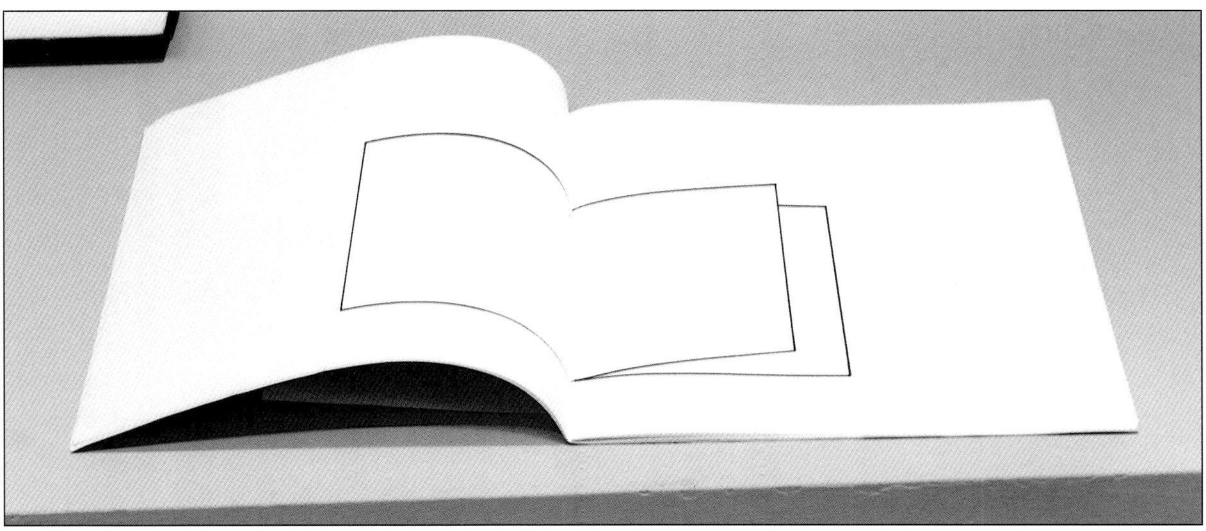

Turning a Page, 1977
Ink on paper, 10 x 10 in.
Collection of Jan van der Marck

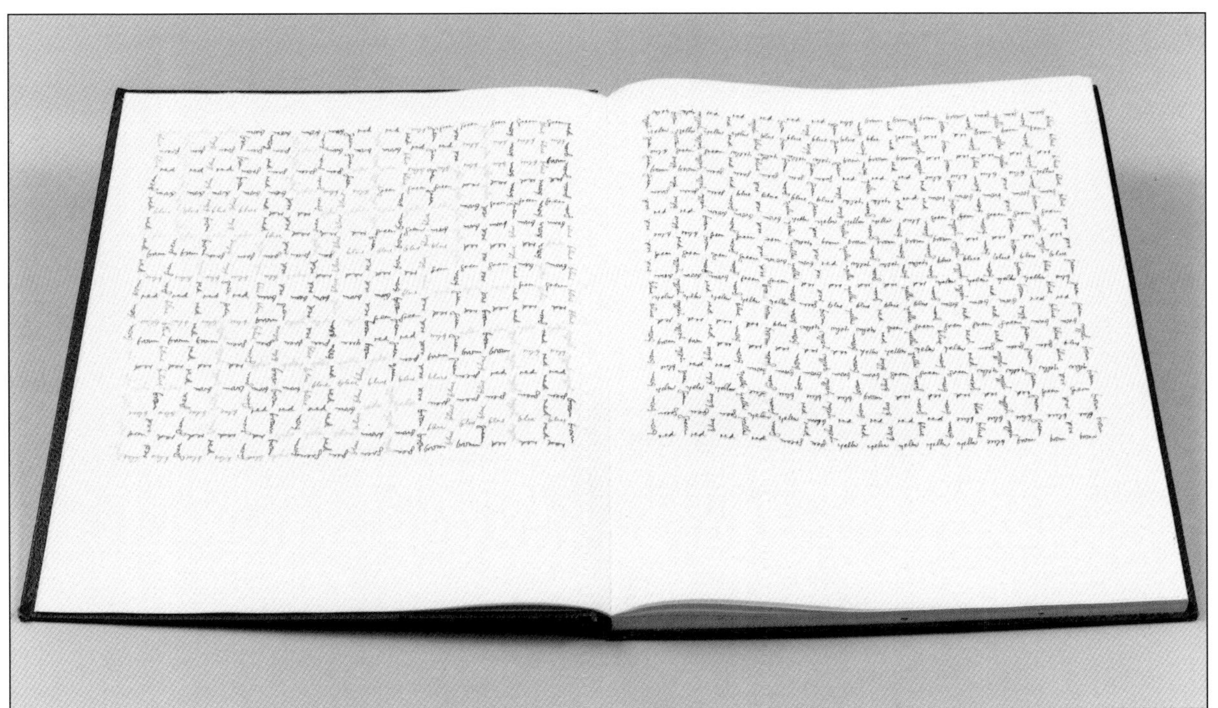

The Book of Rope Drawing: Vowel Grid with Words, 1973
Colored inks on paper, 13 x 9 in.
Collection of the artist

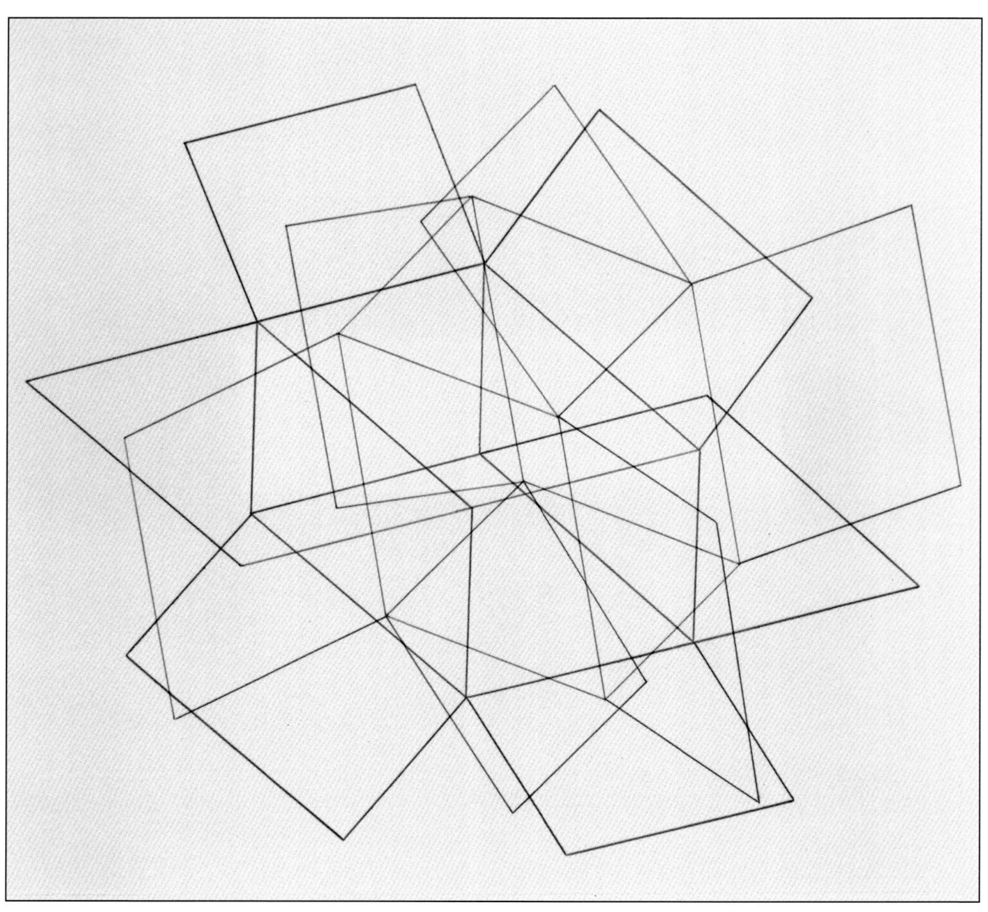

Two Superimposed Open Boxes, 1975
Pencil and colored inks on paper, 23 1/8 x 29 in.
Collection of the artist

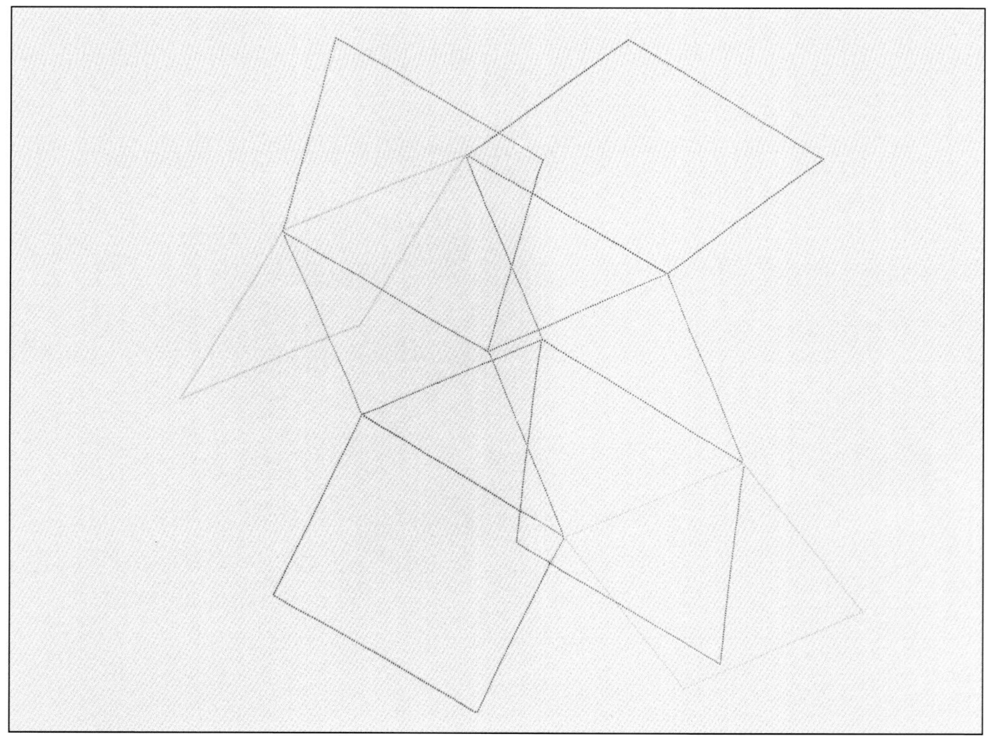

Twelve Planes, 1978
Colored inks on paper, 23 x 29 in.
Collection of the artist

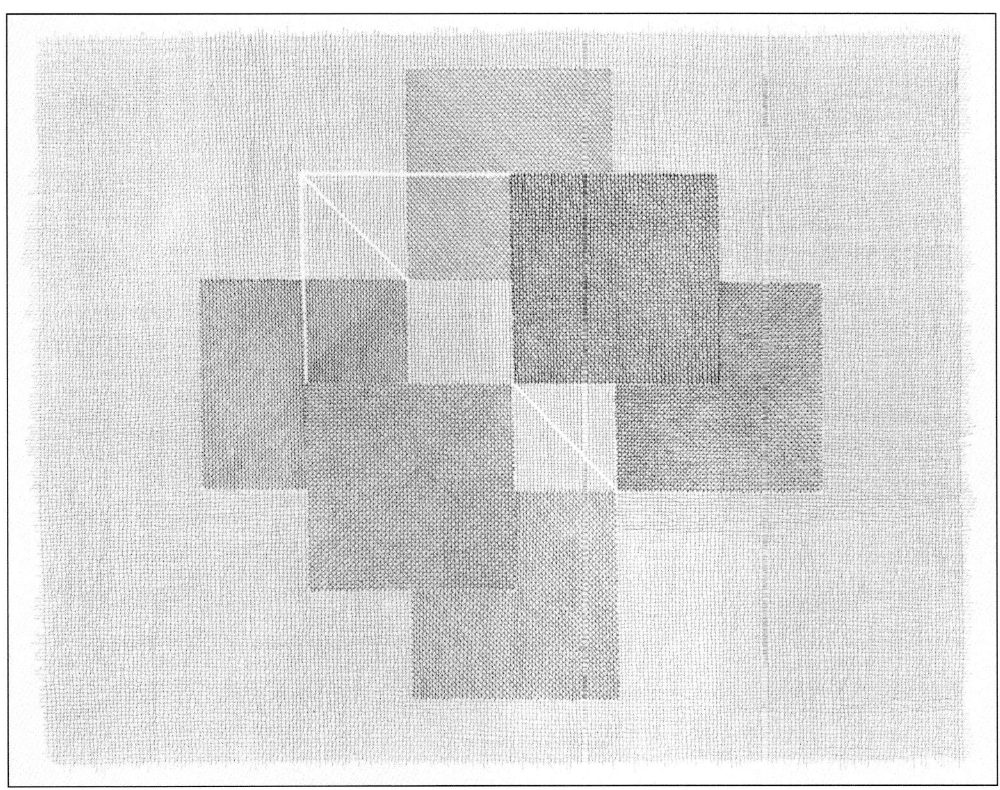

Open Box on Blue Ground, 1986
Colored inks on paper, 23 x 29 in.
Collection of Patrick Merla

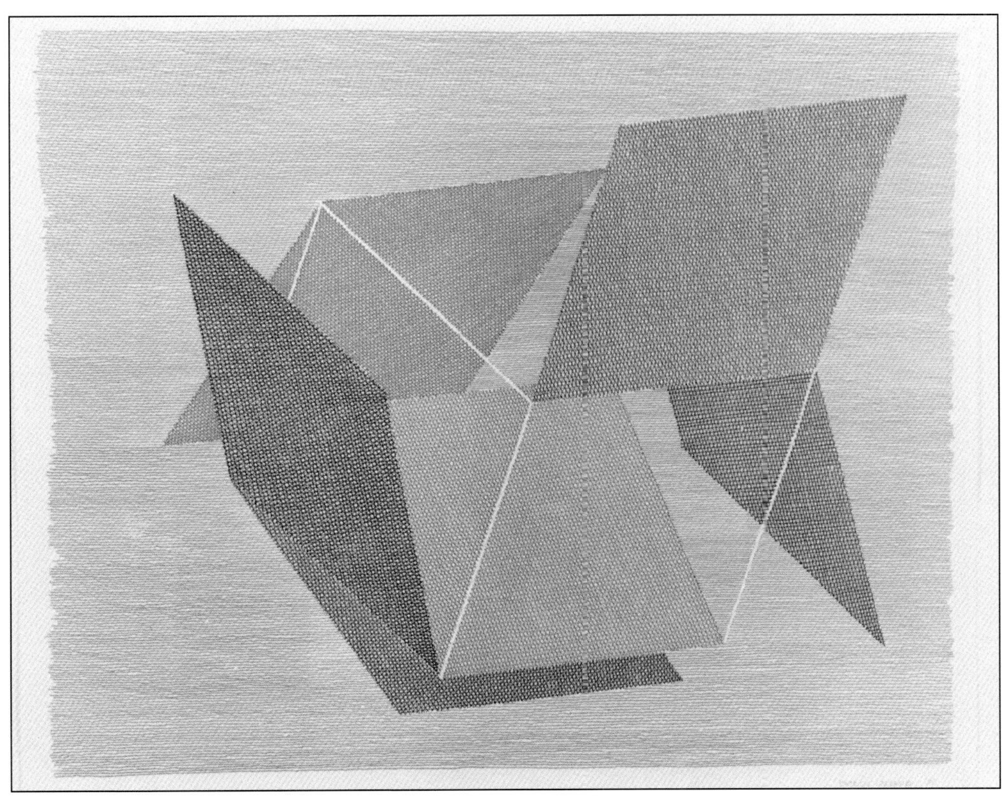

Open Box on Green Ground, 1986
Colored inks on paper, 23 x 29 in.
Collection of Barbara Novak

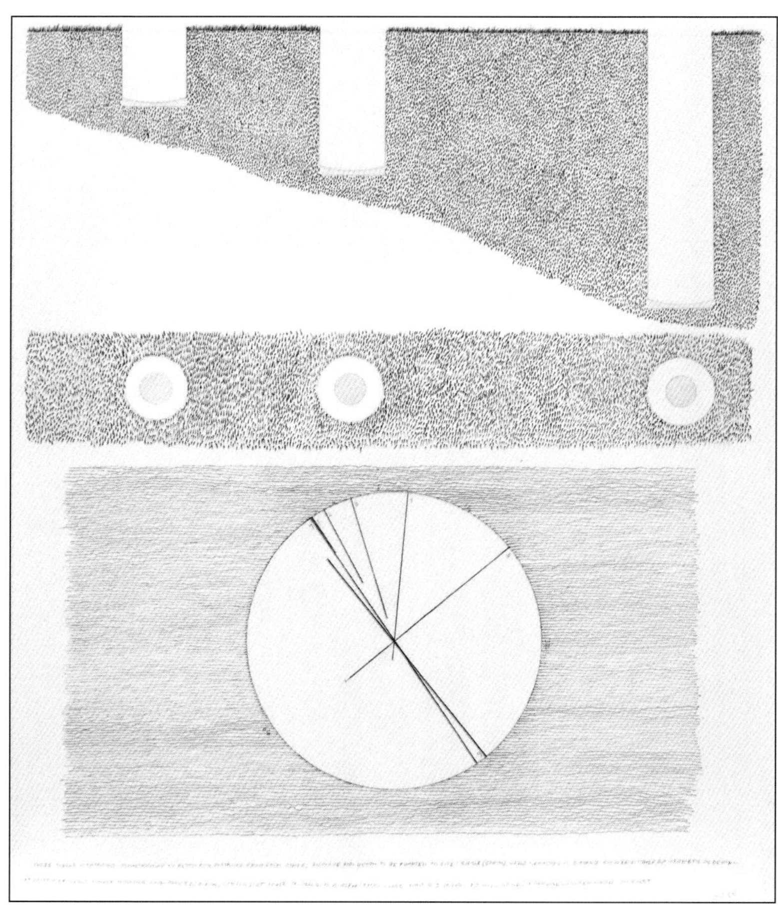

Three Wells, Increasing Geometrically in Depth and Distance from Each Other, 1968
Pencil and colored inks on paper, 29 x 23 1/4 in.
Collection of the artist

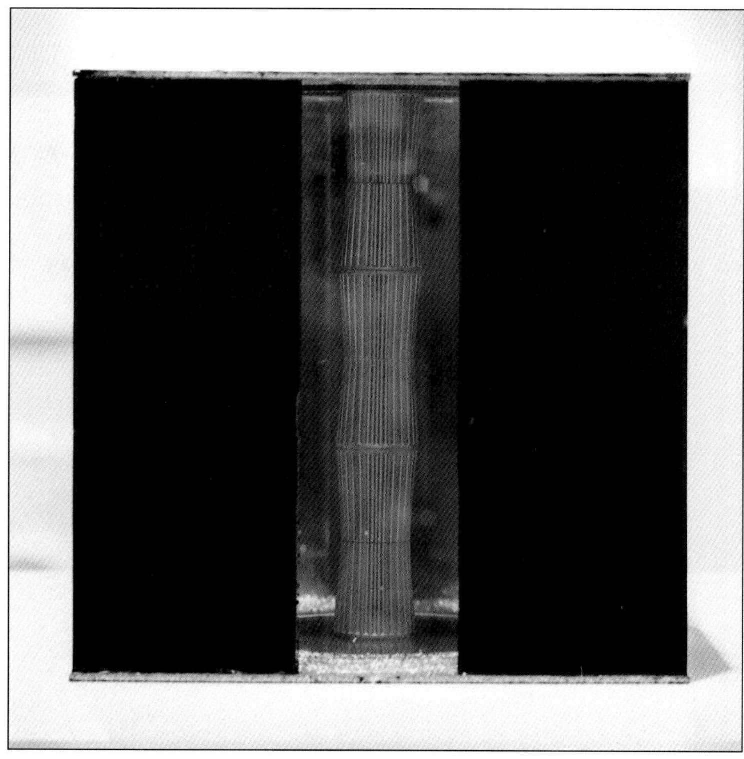

Study for Miami Beach Hotel Foyer, 1968
Glass, mirror, liquitex, bottlecaps, 9 1/2 x 9 3/4 x 9 3/4 in.
Collection of the artist

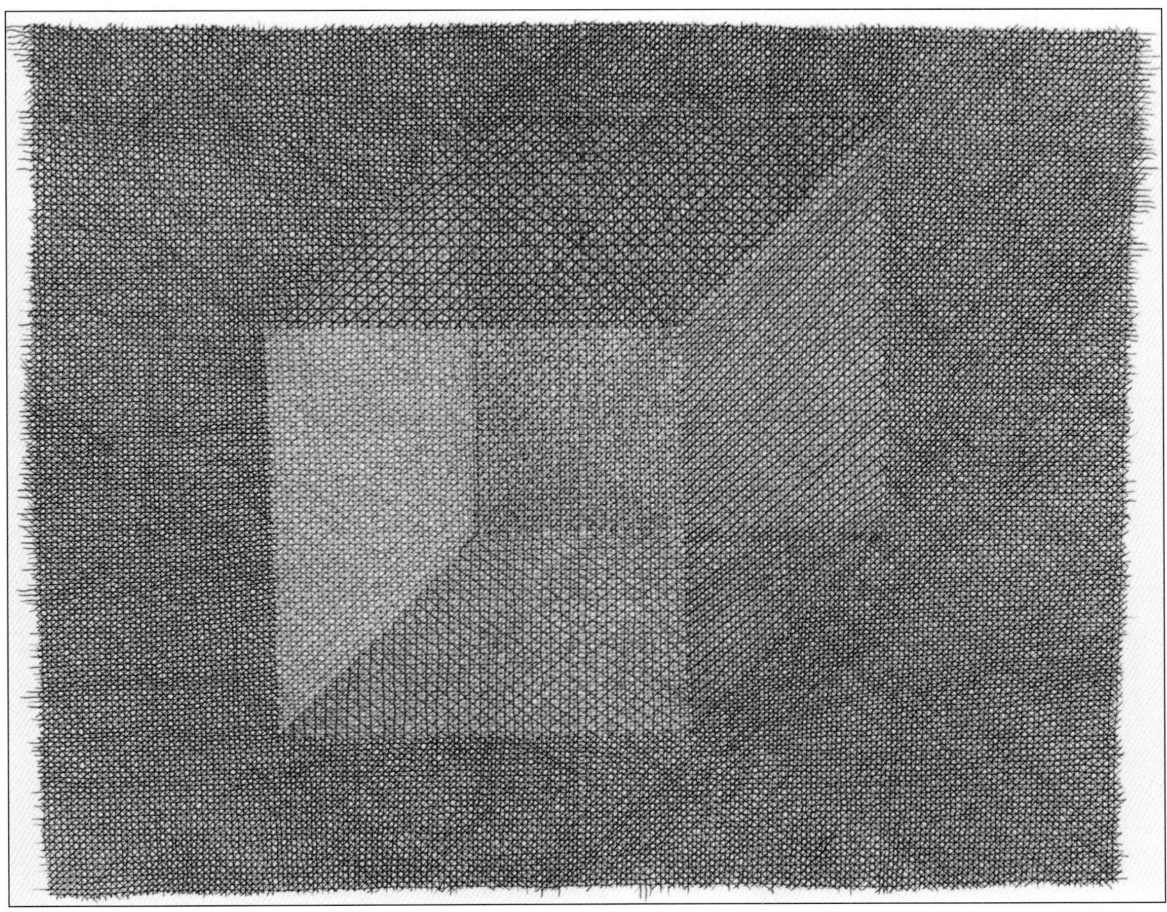

Closed Box: Transparent Cube, 1975
Colored inks on paper, 26 x 40 in.
Collection of the artist

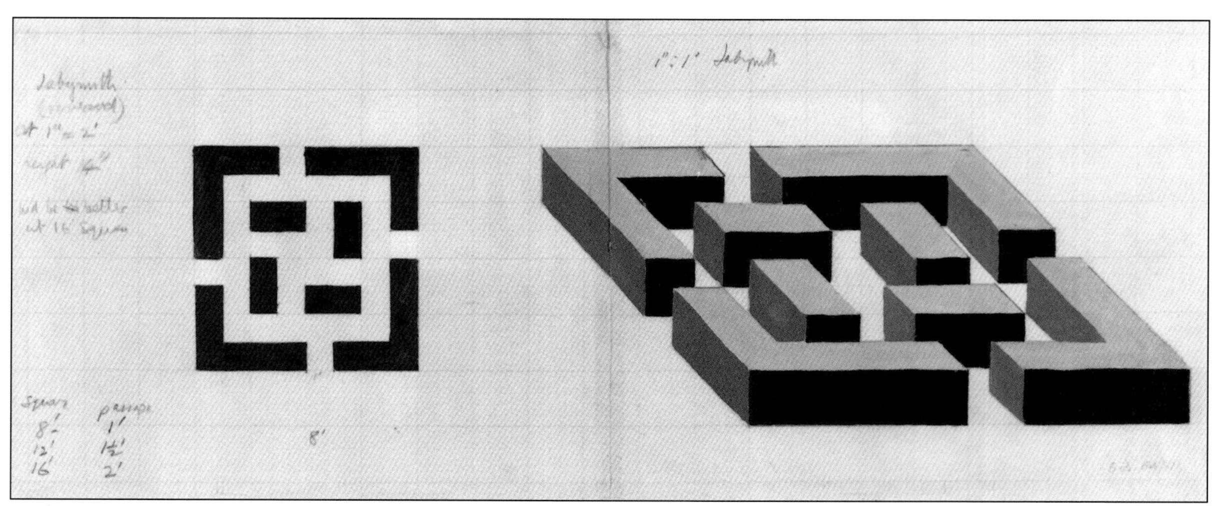

Labyrinth Drawing, Isometric Projection, 1967
Gouache and colored pencils on graph paper, 8½ x 22 in.
Courtesy of the Charles Cowles Gallery

Labyrinth as a Straight Line, 1967–68
Typewriter on paper, each 8½ x 11 in.
Collection of the artist

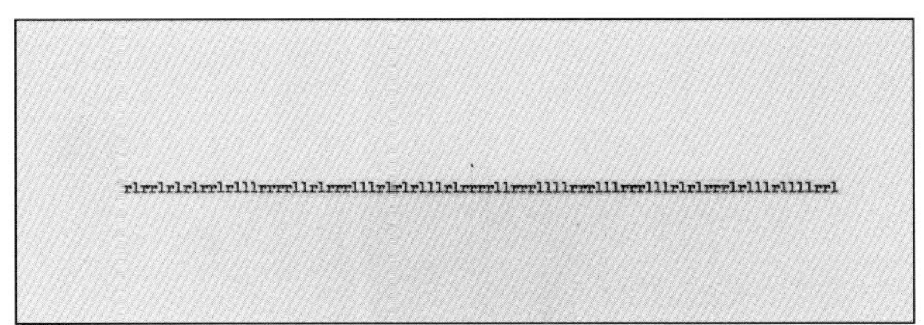

Labyrinth as a Straight Line (Detail)

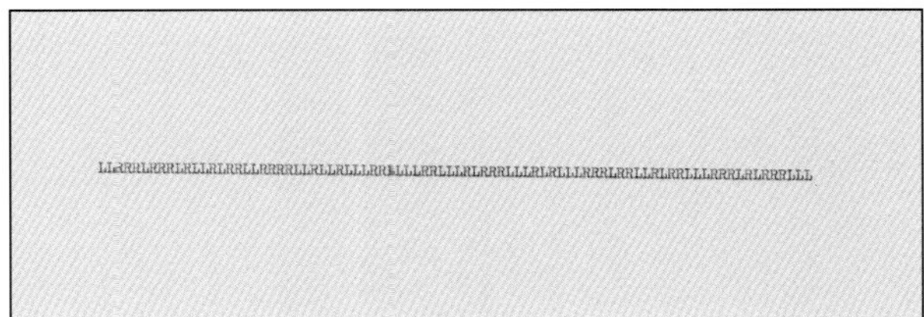

Labyrinth as a Straight Line (Detail)

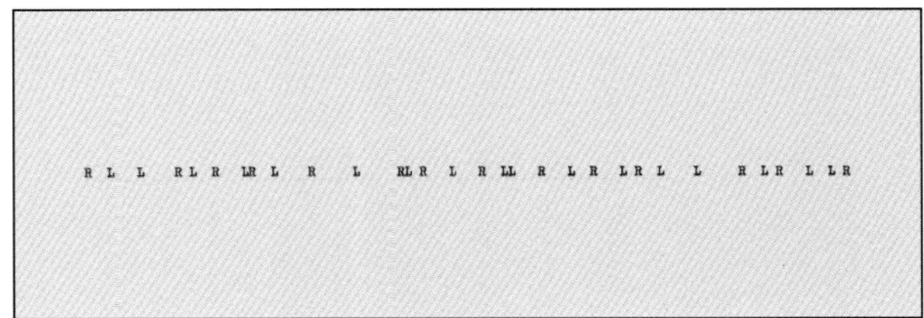

Labyrinth as a Straight Line (Detail)

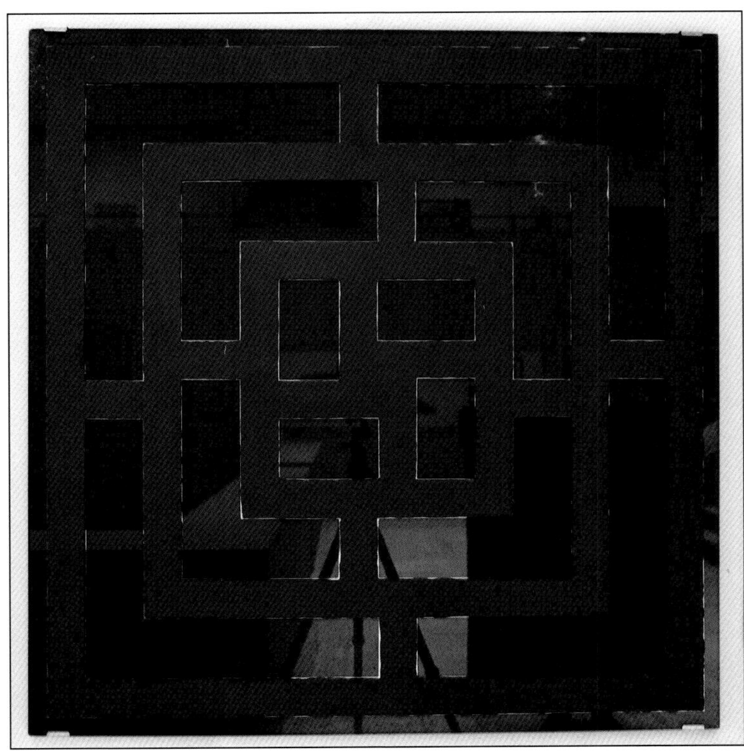

Blue Labyrinth, 1968
Paint on mirror and glass, 36 x 36 in.
Collection of the artist

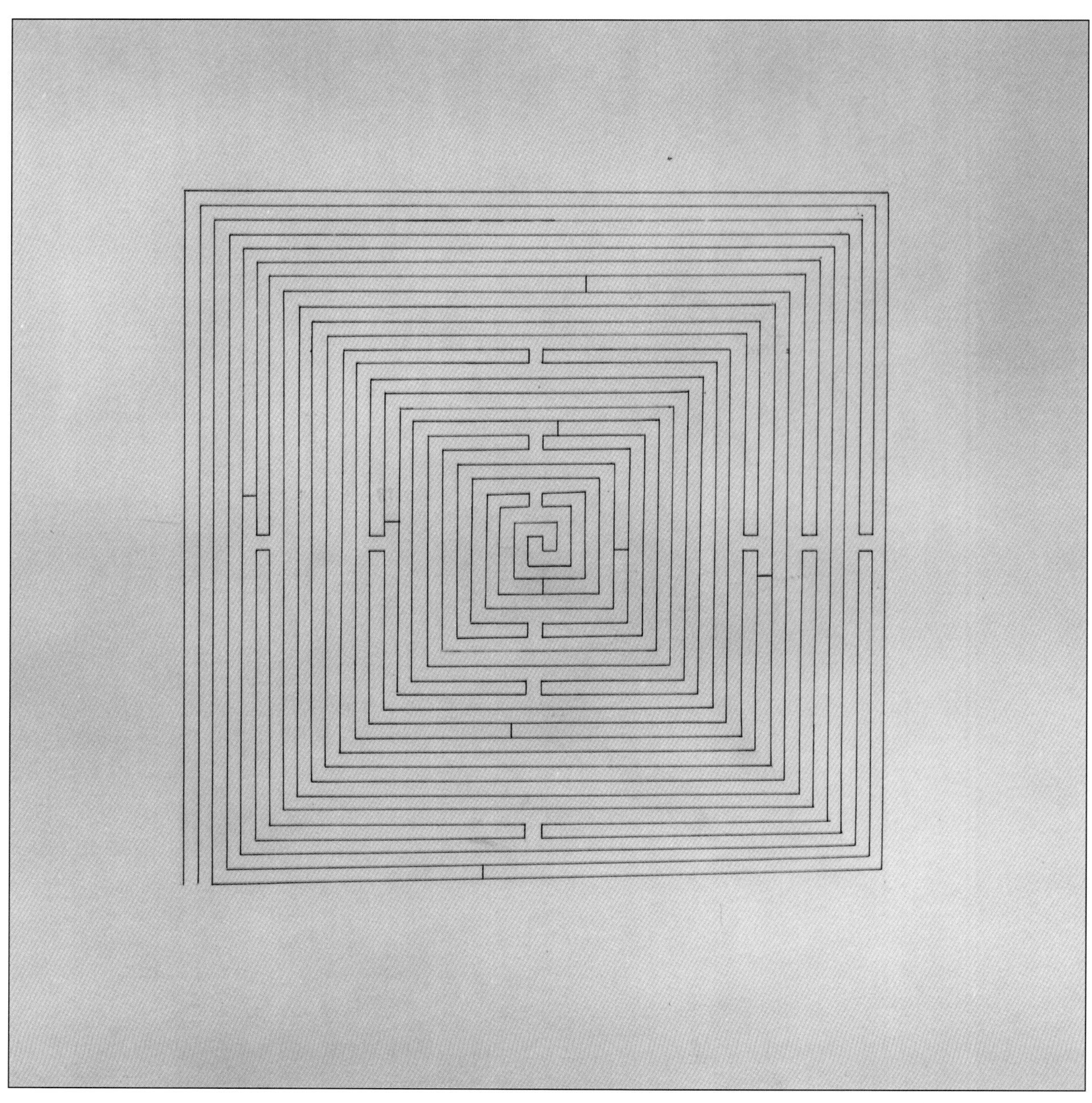

Maze, 1968
Ink on paper, 23 x 29 in.
Collection of the artist

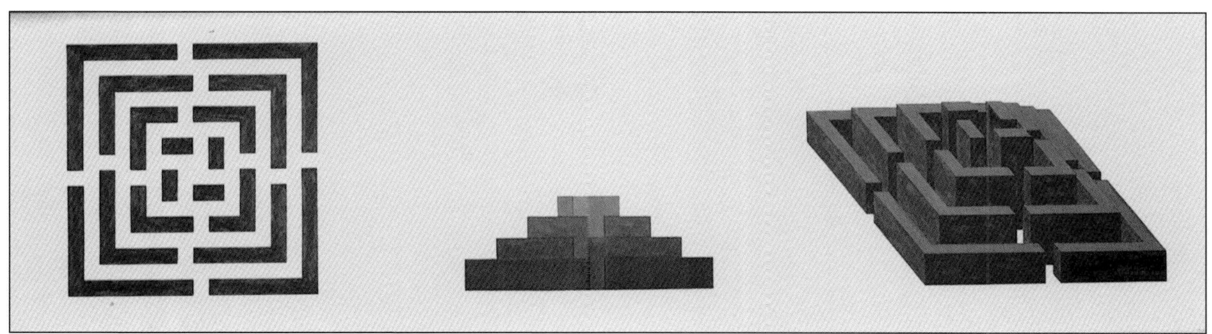

Labyrinth for the Elvehjem Museum, 1992
Pencil and gouache on paper, 44½ x 167 in.
Gift of the artist, 1992.359

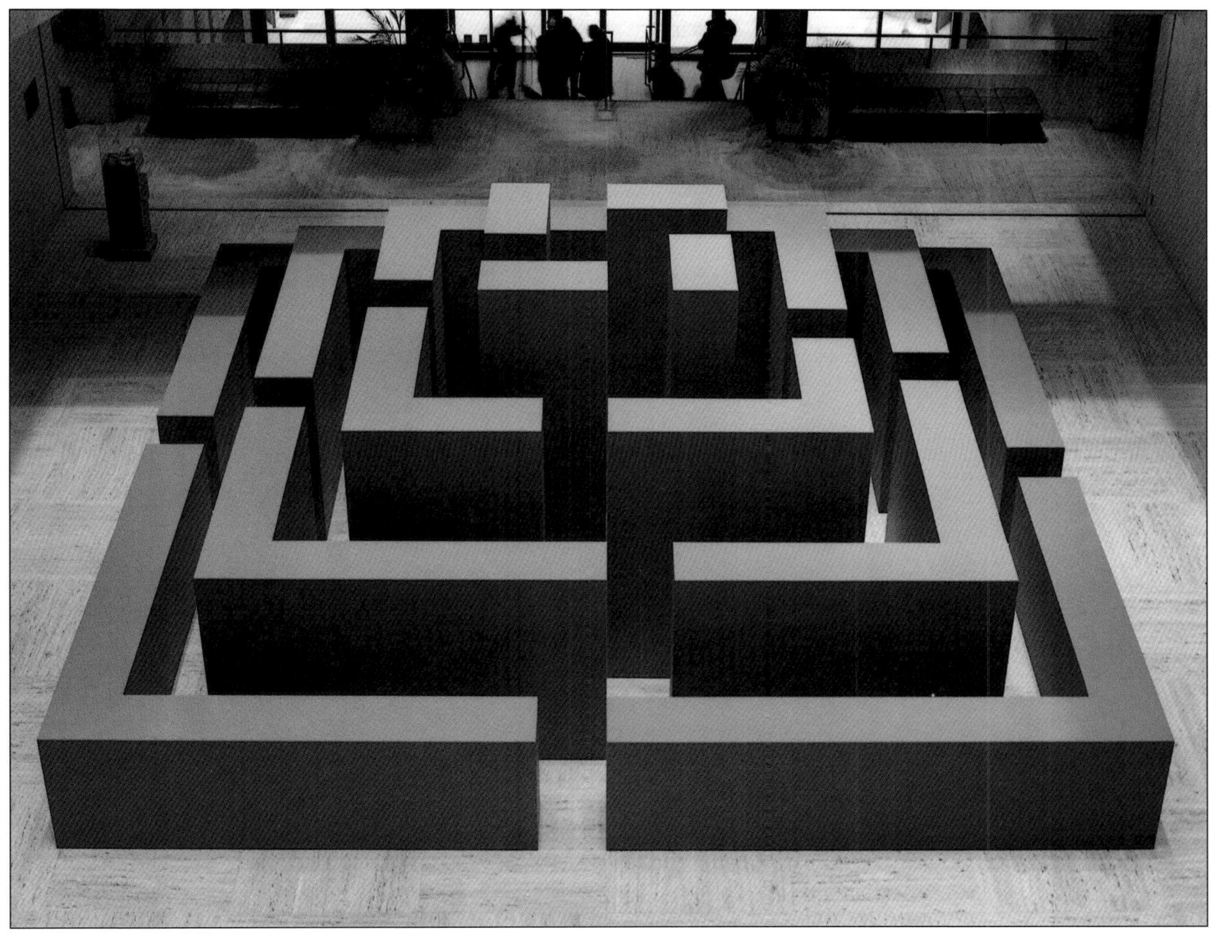

Elvehjem Labyrinth, November 13, 1992–January 10, 1993
Wood, drywall installation, Paige Court of the Elvehjem Museum of Art, 9 x 24 x 24 ft.
Constructed by Tim Coughlin, John Herman, Bruce Marble, Jerry Niesen, Joe Reinmair, and Ray Wahl of the University of Wisconsin–Madison's Physical Plant

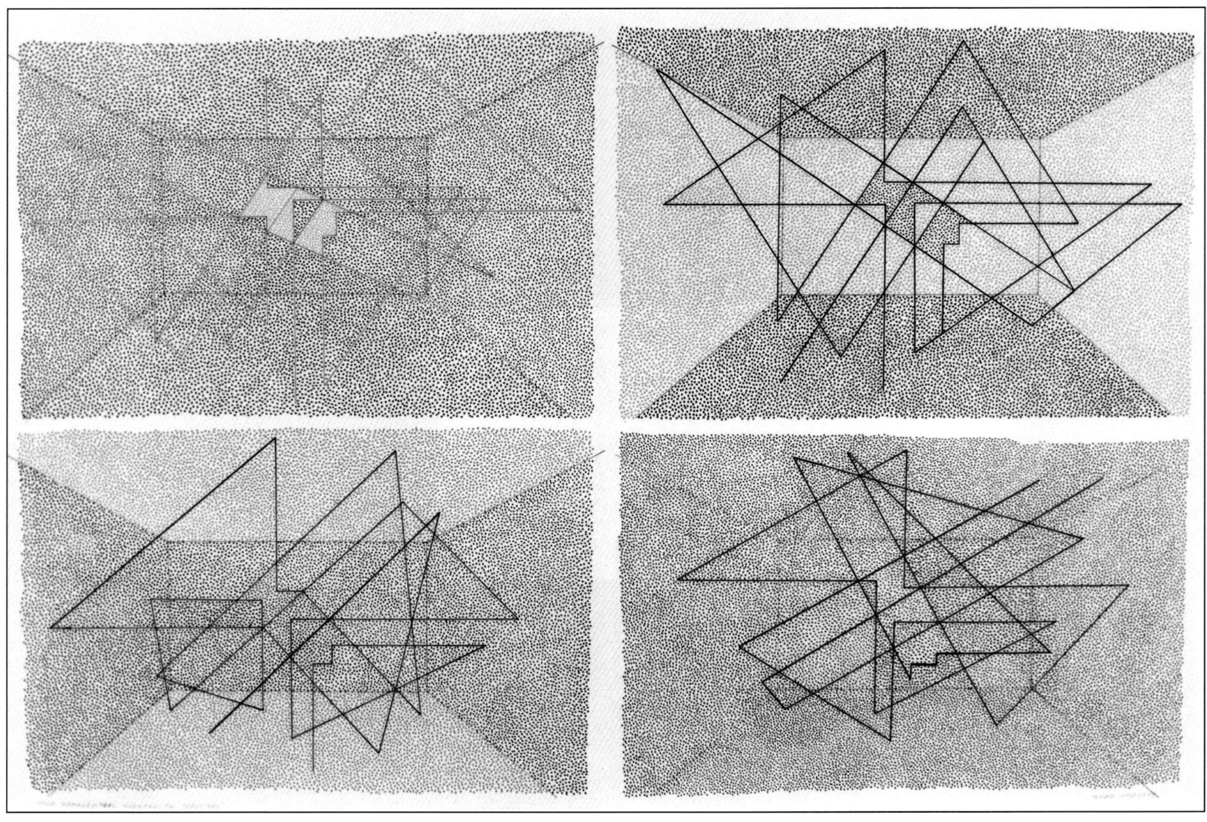

Study for the Purgatory of Humphrey Chimpden Earwicker, Homunculus, Four Spatial /Verbal Propositions, Rope Drawing #73 at the Hyde Gallery, Trinity College, Dublin, February, 1985
Colored inks on paper, 26 x 40 in.
John S. Lord Endowment Fund, Earl O. Vits Endowment Fund, Carolyn T. Anderson Endowment Fund, Walter J. and Cecille Hunt Endowment Fund purchase, 1992.333

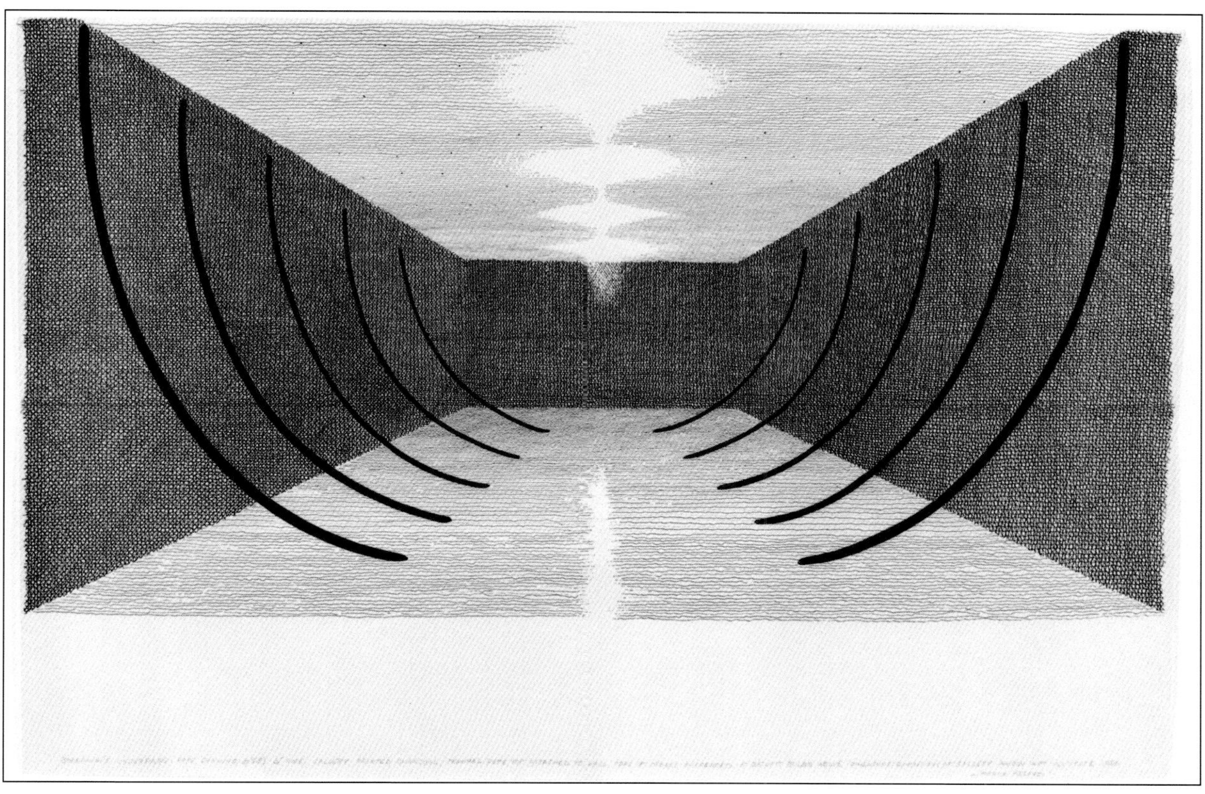

Borromini's Underpass, Rope Drawing #57 at the Akron Art Museum, Akron, Ohio, 1980
Black ink on paper, 28¾ x 43 in.
Courtesy of the Charles Cowles Gallery

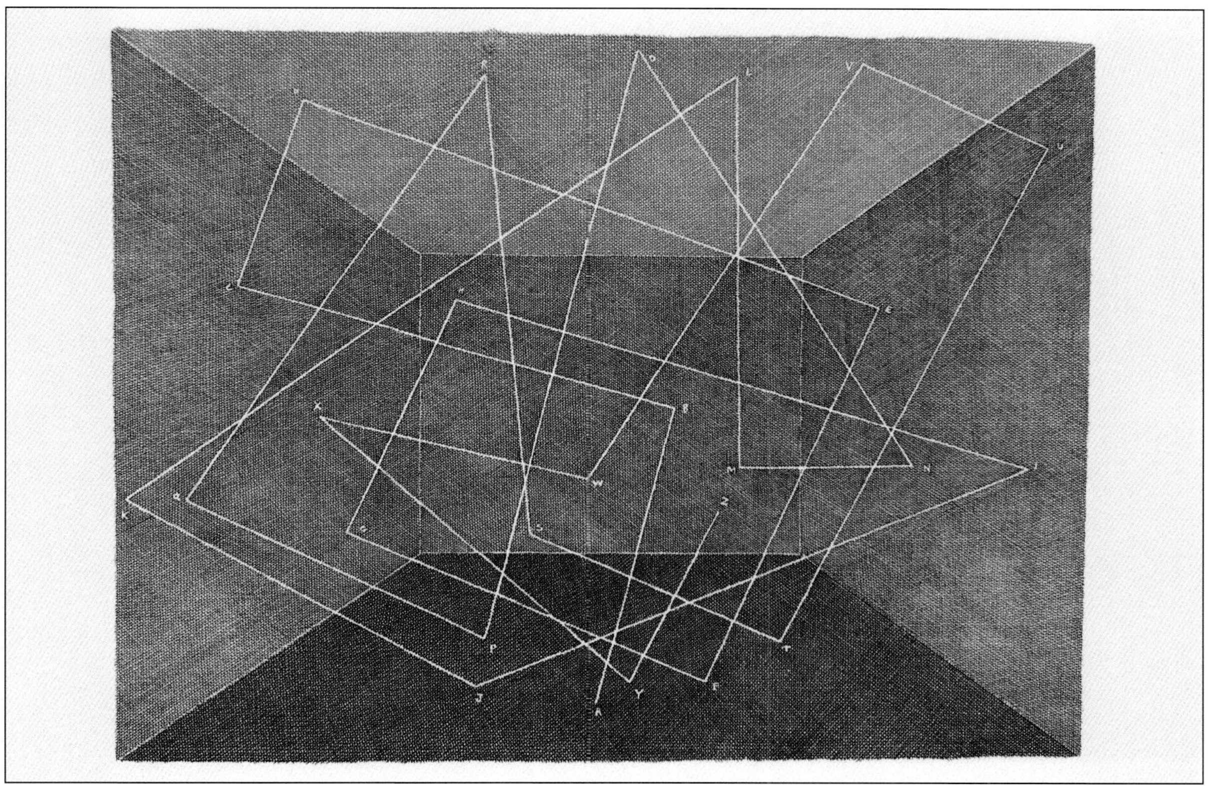

Rimbaud's Cradle, Rope Drawing #67 at the Charles Cowles Gallery, New York, 1983
Colored inks on paper, 26 x 40 in.
Courtesy of the Charles Cowles Gallery

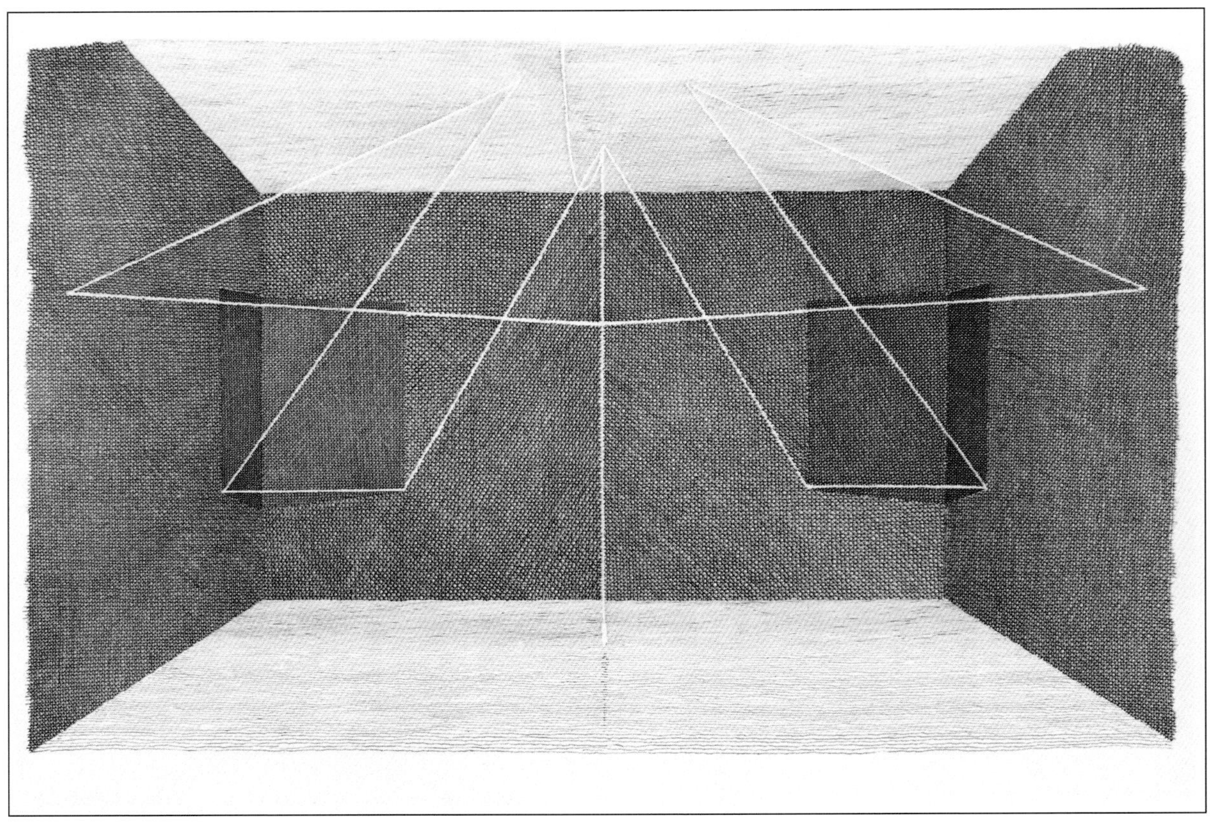

String Quartet, Rope Drawing #64 at the Brooklyn Museum of Art, New York, 1983
Colored inks on paper, 26 x 39¾ in.
Courtesy of Charles Cowles Gallery

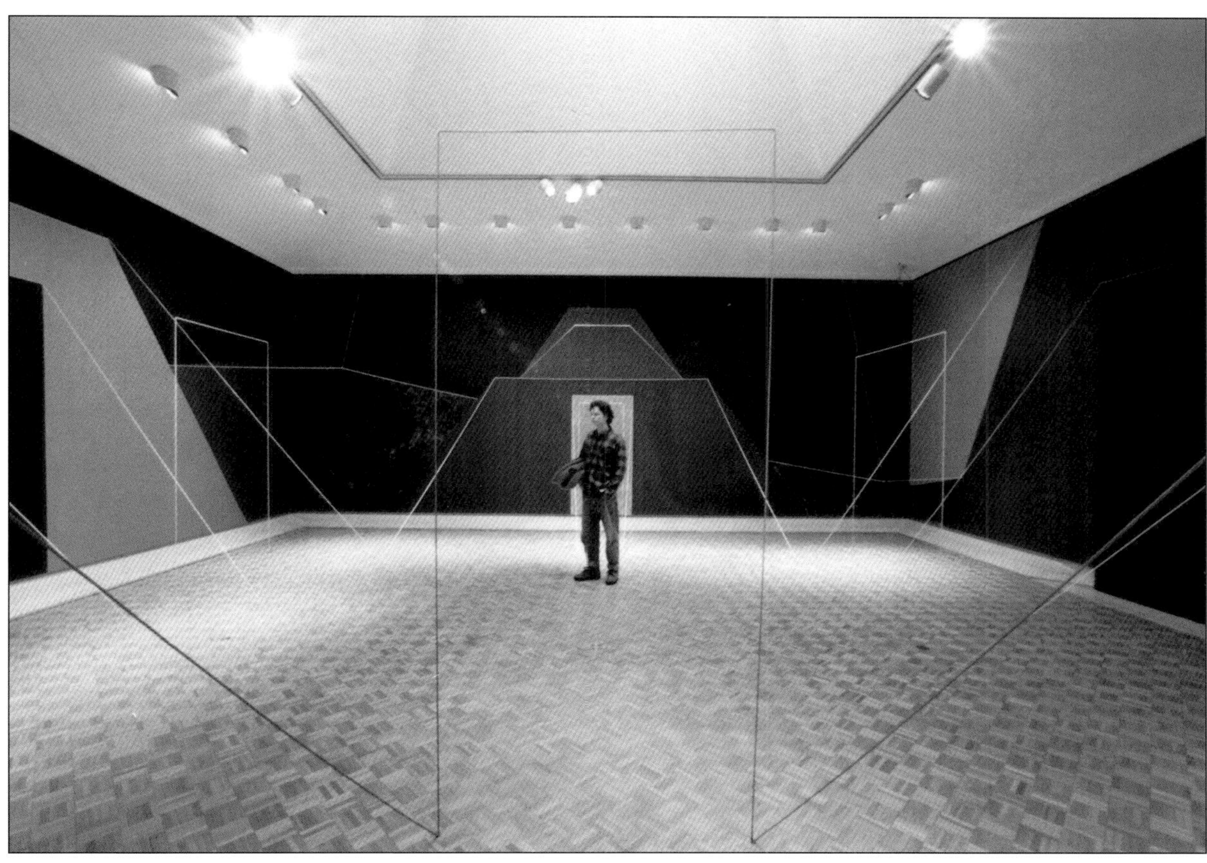

Omphalos, Rope Installation, November 13, 1992 – January 10, 1993
Brittingham Gallery VIII, Elvehjem Museum of Art, Madison, Wisconsin
With assistance of Bruce Conover and Rick Hards

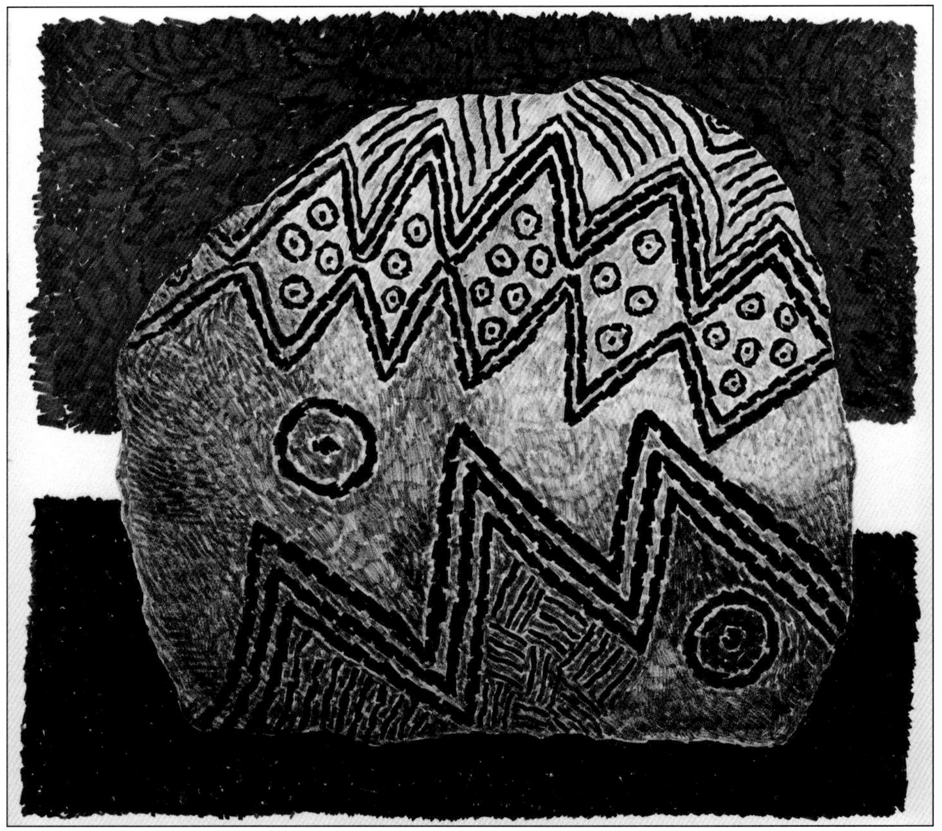

Zigzag Stone, 1983
Watercolor on paper, 45 x 47 in.
Harry and Margaret P. Glicksman Endowment Fund, Cyril W. Nave Endowment Fund,
Alice Drews Gladfelter Memorial Fund purchase, 1992.334

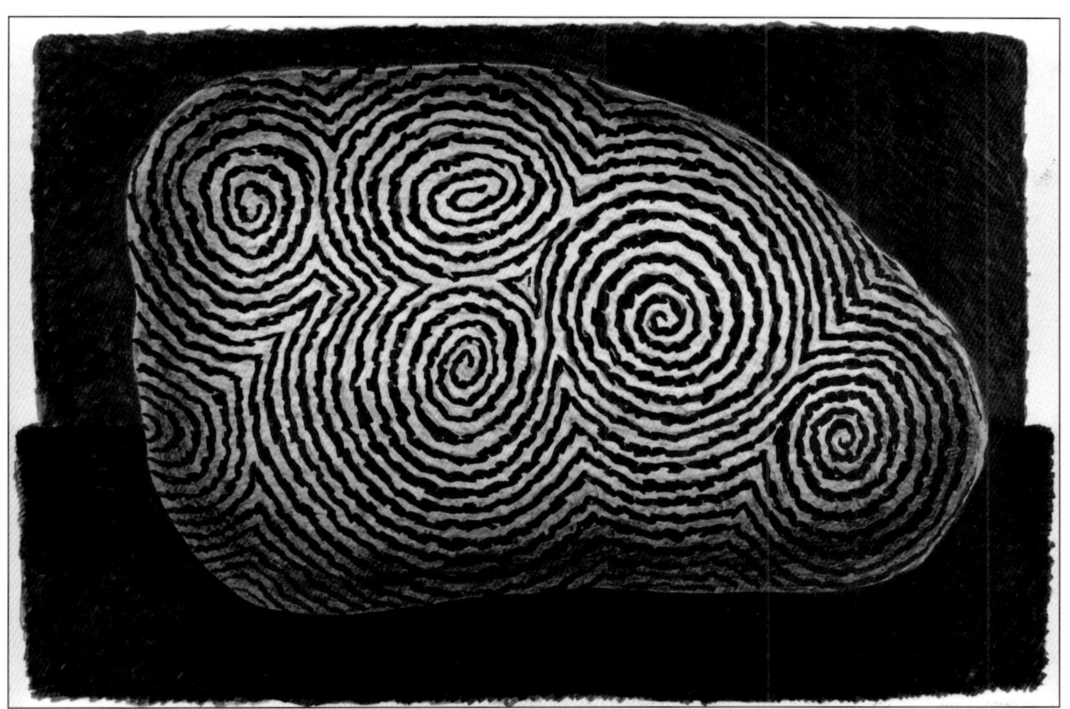

Spiral Stone, 1983
Watercolor on paper, 26 x 40 in.
Collection of Barbara Novak

Patricia Powell, Editor
Greg Anderson, Photographer
Earl J. Madden, Designer
Linda Kietzer, Production Coordinator
University Publications, Compositor
Litho Productions, Printer
The catalogue is typeset in Futura
and printed on Centura Dull paper.